From our Kitchen to Yours

ALL-TIME-FAVORITE RECIPES *From*

North Carolina

COOKS

Dedication

For every cook who wants to create amazing
recipes from the great state of North Carolina.

Appreciation

Thanks to all our North Carolina cooks who shared
their delightful and delicious recipes with us!

Gooseberry Patch
An imprint of Globe Pequot
246 Goose Lane
Guilford, CT 06437
www.gooseberrypatch.com
1 800 854 6673

Copyright 2021, Gooseberry Patch
978-162093-459-3

Do you have a tried & true recipe...tip, craft or
memory that you'd like to see featured in a
Gooseberry Patch cookbook? Visit our website at
www.gooseberrypatch.com and follow the easy steps
to submit your favorite family recipe.

Or send them to us at:

> Gooseberry Patch
> PO Box 812
> Columbus, OH 43216-0812

Don't forget to include the number of servings your
recipe makes, plus your name, address, phone
number and email address. If we select your recipe,
your name will appear right along with it and you'll
receive a FREE copy of the book!

NORTH CAROLINA COOKS

ICONIC NORTH CAROLINA

The beauty of North Carolina flourishes from its breezy coastal beaches to its impressive mountain views. It's no wonder inhabitation in the Tar Heel State has been coveted for over 10,000 years! As one of the first original 13 colonies, with influences such as Native Americans, Southern Appalachian culture, Germany, Switzerland and elsewhere in Europe, North Carolina foods and culture are as unique and diverse as its landscapes!

The variety in cultures has allowed for some of the most delicious and diverse cuisines to derive from North Carolina. Early on, Native Americans in North Carolina consumed turkey and corn. So, one of the most well-known and historic North Carolina foods is cornmeal grits or mush.

Later, around the 1800s, recipes with tomato catsup were consumed in North Carolina. However, the ingredients for the standard North Carolina BBQ sauce vary from family to family. But no matter which BBQ you prefer, this state has it all, along with a delicious history of fresh seafood recipes to go with it!

In this collection from North Carolina cooks, you'll find everything from Almost North Carolina Pulled Pork BBQ, Carolina Garden Stew and Shrimp Soft Tacos to Bacon-Egg Cheddar Waffles and Potato Chip Cookies! We know you will love this collection of tried & true recipes from cooks from all around the great state of North Carolina. Enjoy!

OUR STORY

Back in 1984, our families were neighbors in little Delaware, Ohio. With small children, we wanted to do what we loved and stay home with the kids too. We had always shared a love of home cooking and so, **Gooseberry Patch** was born.

Almost immediately, we found a connection with our customers and it wasn't long before these friends started sharing recipes. Since then we've enjoyed publishing hundreds of cookbooks with your tried & true recipes.

We know we couldn't have done it without our friends all across the country and we look forward to continuing to build a community with you. Welcome to the **Gooseberry Patch** family!

JoAnn & Vickie

TABLE OF CONTENTS

CHAPTER ONE
Bay-Side
BREAKFASTS
6

CHAPTER TWO
Southern-Style
SALADS & SIDES
30

CHAPTER THREE
Raceway
SOUPS & SANDWICHES
52

CHAPTER FOUR
Carolina Mountain
MAINS
76

CHAPTER FIVE
Atlantic Ocean
APPETIZERS & SNACKS
112

CHAPTER SIX
Tar Heel
TREATS & SWEETS
126

CHAPTER ONE

BAY-SIDE

Breakfasts

ENJOY THESE TASTY BREAKFAST RECIPES THAT BRING YOU TO THE TABLE WITH A HEARTY "GOOD MORNING!" AND CARRY YOU THROUGH THE DAY TO TACKLE WHATEVER COMES YOUR WAY.

BRAN & RAISIN MUFFINS

JODY PRESSLEY
CHARLOTTE, NC

Filled with plump raisins, these sweet muffins are perfect for breakfast or tucked into a lunchbox.

2 c. bran and raisin
  cereal
1-1/2 c. milk
1-1/2 c. all-purpose flour
1 t. baking soda
1/4 t. salt
1 egg, beaten
1/2 c. brown sugar,
  packed
2 T. butter, melted

Mix cereal with milk; set aside. In a large bowl, combine remaining ingredients; stir in cereal mixture. Fill lightly greased or paper-lined muffin cups about 2/3 full with batter. Bake at 350 degrees for 20 to 25 minutes.

Makes one dozen.

COCONUT-ORANGE BREAKFAST ROLLS

JEWEL SHARPE
RALEIGH, NC

These sweet rolls are our favorite breakfast when we go camping. Just a few extra ingredients turn store-bought rolls into homemade goodies!

Separate dough into 8 rolls; set icing aside. Place coconut in a dish. Roll each roll in coconut, pressing to make sure sides are covered. Place rolls, cinnamon-side up, into a 9" round cake pan coated with oil. Make a well in the center of each roll; fill with one tablespoon marmalade. Sprinkle rolls with almonds. Bake at 400 degrees for 15 to 20 minutes, until golden. Cool in pan 10 minutes. Mix almond extract into reserved icing. Spread rolls carefully with icing. Serve warm.

Makes 8 servings.

12.4-oz. tube refrigerated cinnamon rolls with icing
3/4 to 1 c. sweetened flaked coconut
1 t. canola oil
1/2 c. orange marmalade
1/4 c. sliced almonds
1/2 to 1 t. almond extract

KITCHEN TIP

A crock of honey butter...so yummy on warm bread, biscuits and muffins. Simply blend together 1/2 cup each of honey and softened butter.

CHERRY-TOP FRENCH TOAST

**BECKY DICKERSON
HENDERSON, NC**

*This breakfast takes me back to my favorite birthday meal! Serve with
a big glass of milk.*

3 eggs

1/4 c. milk

1-1/2 c. corn flake cereal,
finely crushed

21-oz. can cherry pie
filling

8-oz. pkg. cream cheese,
softened

8 slices white or wheat
bread

3 to 4 T. butter

Garnish: powdered
sugar

In a shallow dish, whisk together eggs and milk well. Place crushed cereal in another shallow dish. In a separate bowl, stir together cherry pie filling and cream cheese, mixing well; set aside. Dip bread slices into egg mixture, then into cereal. Melt butter in a skillet over medium- high heat. Add slices, a few at a time; cook until golden on both sides. To serve, add a dollop of cherry mixture to each slice of toast; sprinkle with powdered sugar.

Makes 4 Servings.

BISCUITS & GRAVY CASSEROLE

AUDRA VANHORN-SOREY
COLUMBIA, NC

When I was growing up in a country home, my mother always made homemade biscuits and sawmill gravy on Christmas morning. This recipe tastes homemade, in half the time!

In a heavy skillet, cook sausage over medium heat until browned; do not drain. Sprinkle flour over sausage in pan; stir well. Add milk, salt and pepper; stir to combine. Cook, stirring frequently, just until mixture comes to a boil. If gravy is too thick, stir in a little more milk to desired consistency. Pour gravy into an 11"x7" baking pan coated with non-stick vegetable spray. Arrange unbaked biscuits over gravy. Bake at 400 degrees for 25 minutes, or until biscuits are golden.

Serves 6 to 8.

1/2 lb. ground pork breakfast sausage
3 T. all-purpose flour
2-1/2 c. whole milk
1/2 t. salt
1/2 t. pepper
16-oz. tube refrigerated jumbo flaky biscuits

FRIENDSHIP QUICHE

**LORI COMER
KERNERSVILLE, NC**

This is a wonderful recipe given to me by a friend. The French fried onions really give it a fabulous flavor. I bake this quiche every Christmas and take it to our office...our maintenance man always seems to come by at just the right time for the last slice!

1 refrigerated 9-inch pie crust

1-1/3 c. French fried onions, divided

1-1/2 c. shredded sharp Cheddar cheese

6 eggs, beaten

1 c. half-and-half or milk

1/2 c. bacon bits

Optional: 1/2 green pepper, finely chopped

Unfold pie crust and place in a 9" pie plate. Sprinkle 3/4 cup onions evenly over bottom of crust; sprinkle with cheese. In a medium bowl, whisk together eggs, half-and-half or milk, bacon bits and green pepper, if using. Pour mixture over cheese. Bake at 350 degrees for 30 minutes, or until center tests done. Sprinkle remaining onions on top. Bake an additional 5 minutes, or until golden. Let stand 5 minutes before slicing.

Makes 8 servings.

JUST FOR FUN

Gliding from sand dunes at Kitty Hawk on the Outer Banks, the Wright Brothers made the first successful airplane flights on December 17, 1903. At a museum on the site where it all happened, visitors can see a full-size replica of that first, fragile little airplane.

SMITH FAMILY BREAKFAST BAKE

CHERYLANN SMITH
HILLSBOROUGH, NC

I created this recipe to duplicate one I tasted and loved. Now my kids and husband love it too!

Arrange torn biscuits in a lightly greased 13"x9" baking pan. Top with sausage; set aside. Blend eggs and milk with seasonings. Pour over sausage; sprinkle with cheese. Bake, uncovered, at 350 degrees for 30 minutes, or until golden.

Serves 12.

12-oz. tube refrigerated biscuits, baked and torn

1 lb. ground pork sausage, browned and drained

8 eggs, beaten

2 c. milk

1 sprig fresh rosemary, chopped

1 t. Italian seasoning

1 t. dried basil

1 t. dried oregano

1 t. dried thyme

salt and pepper to taste

8-oz. pkg. shredded Cheddar cheese

MIXED-UP HAM & EGG MUFFINS

AMY THOMASON HUNT
TRAPHILL, NC

These tasty muffins are perfect for brunch alongside a fruit salad.

1 doz. eggs, beaten
1/2 c. onion, diced
1/4 c. green pepper, chopped
1/2 c. mushrooms, chopped
1/4 t. garlic powder
1/2 t. salt
1/4 t. pepper
1/2 lb. cooked ham, diced
1/2 c. shredded Cheddar cheese

In a large bowl, whisk together eggs, vegetables and seasonings. Stir in ham and cheese. Spray 12 muffin cups with non-stick vegetable spray. Spoon egg mixture into muffin cups, filling 1/3 full. Bake at 350 degrees for 20 to 25 minutes.

Makes one dozen.

CINNAMON-PECAN STICKY BUNS

CRYSTAL SHOOK
CATAWBA, NC

A warm, sweet home-baked treat that's ready in a jiffy.

Melt butter in a 9" round cake pan in the oven at 350 degrees; tilt to coat pan. Mix brown sugar, pecans and cinnamon in a small bowl; sprinkle over melted butter. Arrange biscuits in pan with sides touching (biscuits will fit tightly). Bake at 350 degrees for 25 to 30 minutes, until biscuits are golden and centers of biscuits are fully baked. Invert pan immediately onto a serving plate. Spread any remaining topping from pan on top of buns. Serve warm.

Makes 8 buns.

- 1/3 c. butter, sliced
- 1/2 c. brown sugar, packed
- 1/2 c. chopped pecans
- 1 t. cinnamon
- 16-oz. tube refrigerated biscuits

PEANUTTY BREAKFAST WRAP

CRYSTAL SHOOK
CATAWBA, NC

In a hurry every morning? Don't leave home without breakfast!

8-inch whole-wheat
   tortilla
1 T. creamy peanut
   butter
1 T. vanilla yogurt
1 T. honey
1/4 c. granola
1/4 c. blueberries or
   strawberries, or 1/2
   banana, diced

Spread one side of tortilla with peanut butter and yogurt. Drizzle with honey; sprinkle with granola and fruit. Roll up tightly. Serve immediately, or wrap tightly in plastic wrap and refrigerate.

Makes one serving.

APPLE & PEANUT BUTTER CRESCENTS

JEWEL SHARPE
RALEIGH, NC

So easy to make! Delicious for breakfast, or enjoy as a snack.

8-oz. tube refrigerated
   crescent rolls
1/2 c. creamy peanut
   butter
1 T. apricot preserves
1 baking apple, cored
   and cut into 8 slices
1 egg, beaten

Separate rolls into 8 triangles. Spread with peanut butter and preserves. Place one apple slice on the wide end of each triangle; roll up loosely. Place crescents on an ungreased baking sheet, apple-side up. Brush with beaten egg. Bake at 375 degrees for 10 to 13 minutes, until golden.

Makes 8 servings.

HOT DOG GRAVY & BISCUITS

JENNIFER BOWER
WINSTON-SALEM, NC

One of my most favorite Saturday breakfasts. Whenever I had a slumber party, my mom would make this breakfast...my friends thought it was terribly delicious!

Heat oil over medium heat in a large skillet. Add hot dogs and brown lightly. Stir in flour and pepper; mix well. Stir in milk; bring to a boil. Cook and stir until thickened; remove from heat. Serve over biscuits.

Serves 4.

2-1/2 **T.** oil
16-oz. pkg. hot dogs,
  sliced 1/4-inch thick
3 **T.** all-purpose flour
1/8 t. pepper
1-1/2 c. milk
4 biscuits, split

PRESENTATION

A fresh-baked quiche looks so pretty presented in an old-fashioned glass pie plate. Wrap it up in clear cellophane and use a favorite black & white photo for a gift tag.

CHRISTMAS MORN SAUSAGE BAKE

SHEILA LOWANS
BAHAMA, NC

My mother used to fix this casserole for Christmas morning every year. Now I fix it for my own family, and I hope to pass it on to my girls too.

6 slices bread

1 lb. ground pork breakfast sausage, browned, drained and divided

1 c. shredded Swiss cheese

1 c. shredded Cheddar cheese

3 eggs, beaten

2 c. milk

salt to taste

Place 3 bread slices in the bottom of a greased 1-1/2 quart casserole dish. Spread half of sausage over bread; spread half of cheeses over sausage. Repeat layers. Beat eggs, milk and salt together; pour over top. Bake, uncovered, at 350 degrees for one hour.

Serves 6 to 8.

BACON-EGG CHEDDAR WAFFLE

AMY BRADSHER
ROXBORO, NC

We love our BECW! My kids think it's hilarious to eat waffles with their hands, and it always makes them giggle. It's a fun breakfast at home or on the go. Save time...make 'em ahead and freeze!

Whisk eggs and milk together. Melt one teaspoon butter in a small skillet over low heat. Add 1/4 of egg mixture and cook omelet-style; top with 2 tablespoons cheese when nearly done. Repeat, making 3 more omelets. Meanwhile, make Waffles. To assemble sandwiches, slide one omelet between 2 waffles; top with several slices bacon. Slice in half along the waffle's divider lines. Serve immediately, or wrap with wax paper, place in plastic zipping bags and freeze.

Waffles:

In a large bowl, whisk together all ingredients until smooth. Add batter by 1/2 cupfuls to a preheated waffle iron; cook according to manufacturer's directions.

Serves 4 to 6.

8 eggs, beaten
1/3 c. milk
4 t. butter, divided
1/2 c. shredded Cheddar cheese, divided
1 lb. bacon, crisply cooked

WAFFLES
3-1/2 c. white whole-wheat flour
4 eggs, beaten
3 c. buttermilk
1/4 c. butter, melted
2 t. baking soda
1 t. salt

BREAKFAST IN A BUN

AMY CASSIDY
MORGANTON, NC

A fast way to eat breakfast...wrap it up and eat it on the go!

4 eggs, beaten
1 to 2 T. milk
2 to 3 t. butter
4 hot dog buns, warmed
Optional: 1/4 c.
  mayonnaise
4 slices American
  cheese
8 brown & serve
  breakfast sausage
  links, cooked

Whisk together eggs and milk. In a skillet over low heat, scramble eggs in butter to desired doneness. Meanwhile, spread warmed buns with mayonnaise, if desired; top each bun with one cheese slice and 2 sausage links. Spoon eggs into buns.

Serves 4.

BANANA-MANGO SOY SMOOTHIE

SHIRL PARSONS
CAPE CARTERET, NC

A cool refreshing pick-me-up drink... especially good for those who can't tolerate milk!

2 c. vanilla or plain soy
  milk
2 to 3 bananas, sliced
  and frozen
6 mangoes, peeled,
  pitted, cubed and
  frozen
1 T. honey, or to taste

Combine all ingredients in a blender. Blend on high setting until smooth and frothy. Pour into tall glasses.

Makes 6 servings.

PUMPKIN FRENCH TOAST BAKE

AUDRA VANHORN-SOREY
COLUMBIA, NC

This recipe is delightful on a cool fall morning. Just pull it from the fridge and bake...the delicious aroma will bring everyone to the breakfast table!

Spread bread cubes in a greased 13"x9" baking pan; set aside. In a large bowl, whisk together eggs, milk, pumpkin, 1-1/2 teaspoons spice and vanilla. Pour evenly over bread; press down with spoon until bread is saturated. Cover and refrigerate overnight. In the morning, uncover and top with brown sugar, remaining spice and pecans, if desired. Bake, uncovered, at 350 degrees for 35 to 45 minutes, until golden. Serve with maple syrup.

Serves 10.

1 loaf crusty French bread, cubed

7 eggs, beaten

2 c. milk

1/2 c. canned pumpkin

2 t. pumpkin pie spice, divided

1 t. vanilla extract

3-1/2 T. brown sugar, packed

Optional: 1/2 c. chopped pecans

Garnish: maple syrup

FAMILY-TIME CONVERSATION

A protected herd of wild horses lives at Corolla on the Outer Banks, said to be the descendants of mustangs left behind by Spanish explorers in the 15th century. The Corolla Wild Horse was named the official state horse of North Carolina in 2010, following a letter-writing campaign by schoolchildren.

BLUEBERRY BUCKWHEAT PANCAKES

**LYNNETTE JONES
EAST FLAT ROCK, NC**

Buckwheat pancakes just taste like fall! Feel free to use your own favorite fresh or frozen berries.

1-1/2 c. buckwheat flour
1/2 t. baking powder
1/2 t. baking soda
1/4 t. salt
1 c. buttermilk
2 egg whites, beaten
1 egg, beaten
1 T. honey
1 T. canola oil
1 t. vanilla extract
1 c. blueberries, thawed
   if frozen
Garnish: maple syrup,
   fresh fruit

In a bowl, mix flour, baking powder, baking soda and salt. In a separate bowl, stir together buttermilk, egg whites, egg, honey, oil and vanilla. Add buttermilk mixture to flour mixture; stir well. Gently fold in blueberries. Heat a lightly greased skillet over medium heat. Add batter by 1/4 cupfuls. Cook until bubbles appear on top, about 1-1/2 minutes. Turn; cook other side until golden, about 1-1/2 minutes. Top with maple syrup or more fresh fruit, as desired.

Makes 4 servings.

MAKE-AHEAD PUMPKIN PIE FRENCH TOAST

JENNIFER YANDLE
INDIAN TRAIL, NC

This is a great Sunday morning breakfast...it can bake while you get ready for church. It's also super-easy for husbands to whip up, so Mom can sleep in just a bit on Saturday morning!

Arrange bread slices in bottom of a greased 13"x9" baking pan. Whisk together eggs, milk, half-and-half, egg substitute, spice, vanilla and salt. Stir in brown sugar; pour mixture over bread slices. Refrigerate, covered, overnight. Dot top with butter and bake, uncovered, at 350 degrees for 40 to 45 minutes.

Makes 8 servings.

1 loaf French, Italian, challah or Hawaiian bread, cut into 1-inch slices

3 eggs, beaten

1-1/2 c. milk

1 c. half-and-half

1/2 c. egg substitute

1 T. pumpkin pie spice

1 t. vanilla extract

1/4 t. salt

1/2 c. brown sugar, packed

1 to 2 T. butter, sliced

SWEET TWISTS

MARY JANE TOLMAN
ROCKY MOUNT, NC

These go great with a tall glass of cold milk for dunking.

1 env. active dry yeast
1/4 c. warm water
3-3/4 c. all-purpose flour
1-1/2 t. salt
1 c. butter
2 eggs, beaten
1/2 c. sour cream
3 t. vanilla extract, divided
1-1/2 c. sugar

Dissolve yeast in very warm water, 110 to 115 degrees; set aside. Mix flour and salt in a large bowl; cut in butter until coarse crumbs form. Blend in eggs, sour cream, one teaspoon vanilla and yeast mixture; cover and chill overnight. Combine sugar and remaining vanilla. Sprinkle 1/2 cup vanilla-sugar mixture on a flat surface; roll out dough into a 16-inch by 8-inch rectangle. Sprinkle one tablespoon of vanilla-sugar mixture over dough; fold dough over and roll into a rectangle again. Continue sprinkling mixture, folding and rolling until no vanilla-sugar remains. Cut dough into 4-inch by 1-inch strips; twist strips and place on greased baking sheets. Bake at 350 degrees for 15 to 20 minutes.

Makes 2 dozen.

JUST FOR FUN

In 1898, the first Pepsi-Cola was created and served in New Bern. Pharmacist Caleb Bradham created it as a digestive aid, but it soon became popular as a refreshing cold beverage.

NANNIE'S OATMEAL SCONES

FERN WHITTEMORE
WINSTON-SALEM, NC

This is an old recipe...I'm 90 now, was married at 27! Nannie used to make these scones every Sunday morning. I missed them when I married and moved from Canada to North Carolina, until she sent me the recipe.

Combine all ingredients in a large bowl; mix well with your hands. Turn out dough onto a floured surface; press into a square, 1/2 to 3/4-inch thick. Cut into 4 squares; cut each square in half on the diagonal to make 8 pieces. Place on a parchment paper-lined baking sheet. Bake at 325 degrees for 25 minutes, or until golden. Serve with butter.

Makes 8 scones.

1-1/2 c. all-purpose flour
1 c. quick-cooking oats, uncooked
1 c. brown sugar, packed
1/2 c. butter, softened
1/2 t. baking soda
1/2 c. buttermilk
Optional: 1/2 c. raisins

EGGS ITALIANA

MIA ROSSI
CHARLOTTE, NC

A deliciously different brunch dish.

Set aside 3 cheese slices; chop remaining cheese and place in a large bowl. Add eggs, milk and pepper; whisk well. Stir in remaining ingredients except butter. Brush a slow cooker with butter. Pour egg mixture into slow cooker. Cover and cook on low setting for 3 to 3-1/2 hours. Arrange reserved cheese slices on top. Cover and cook an additional 15 minutes, or just until cheese is melted.

Serves 6.

1/2 lb. thinly sliced provolone cheese, divided
10 eggs, beaten
1 c. milk
1/2 t. pepper
1/4 lb. deli sliced prosciutto or ham, chopped
1/2 c. roasted red peppers, drained and chopped
1/2 c. canned artichokes, drained and thinly sliced
1 T. butter, melted

HASHBROWN BREAKFAST SURPRISE

SUSAN JOHNSON
LITTLE SWITZERLAND, NC

Although this is a Christmas morning recipe, I often fix this during the week, then slice, flash-freeze and store in a freezer bag. Take one slice right out of the freezer, microwave on high for 3 minutes and you have a good hot breakfast meal in a jiffy.

30-oz. pkg. frozen southern-style diced hashbrown potatoes, thawed

9.6-oz. pkg. precooked pork sausage crumbles

1/2 onion, finely chopped

1/2 green pepper, finely chopped

16-oz. pkg. shredded Mexican-blend cheese

1 doz. eggs, well beaten

Spray a 13"x9" glass baking pan with non-stick vegetable spray. Layer ingredients in pan in the order listed, pouring eggs evenly over all. Bake, uncovered, at 350 degrees for 55 minutes, or until set. Cool for 5 minutes; cut into squares.

Serves 8.

GINGERBREAD BISCUITS

KITTY THOMASON BROWN
TRAPHILL, NC

*I make these for my family every Christmas. We think they are
exceptionally good...I hope you'll try them!*

In a bowl, sift together 2-1/4 cups flour, baking soda,
salt and spices; set aside. In a separate large bowl,
blend margarine, sugar and egg. Add flour mixture
and mix well; stir in molasses and buttermilk. Stir
in enough of remaining flour to make a stiff dough.
Cover and refrigerate for 8 hours or overnight. On
a floured surface, roll out dough to 1/8-inch thick;
cut out with a biscuit cutter. Place on lightly greased
baking sheets. Bake at 350 degrees for 8 to 12
minutes.

Makes 2 dozen.

5 c. all-purpose flour,
  divided
1 t. baking soda
1/2 t. salt
1 t. cinnamon
1 t. ground ginger
1/4 t. ground cloves
1/2 c. margarine,
  softened
1/2 c. sugar
1 egg, beaten
3/4 c. molasses
1 c. buttermilk

KITCHEN TIP

For hosting a stress-free brunch, focus on
make-ahead meals like baked French toast
and egg casseroles. Save recipes that need
to be cooked on the spot, like pancakes and
omelets, for smaller family breakfasts.

AMY'S AWESOME SAUSAGE RING

AMY THOMASON HUNT
TRAPHILL, NC

This is a must-have at Thanksgiving, Christmas and gal-time gatherings. For a great brunch dish, spoon scrambled eggs into the center of the ring after it's baked and onto a serving platter.

1 lb. ground pork breakfast sausage

1 green pepper, finely diced

3/4 c. onion, finely diced

1 lb. frozen bread dough, thawed

grated Parmesan cheese and garlic salt to taste

8-oz. pkg. shredded mozzarella cheese

Garnish: warm pizza sauce or sausage gravy for dipping

Brown sausage in a skillet over medium heat, adding pepper and onion during the last few minutes of cooking; drain. Meanwhile, on a lightly floured surface, spread dough into a 15-inch by 10-inch rectangle. Sprinkle dough with Parmesan cheese and garlic salt. Spoon sausage mixture onto dough; spread mixture to within one inch of edges of dough. Top with mozzarella cheese. Roll up, starting on one long edge; form into a ring. Place dough ring in a Bundt® pan sprayed with non- stick vegetable spray; pinch the ends together. Top with additional Parmesan cheese. Bake at 350 degrees for 20 to 25 minutes, until golden. Turn out onto a serving platter; serve with desired dipping sauce.

Serves 8 to 10.

EASY BREAKFAST STRATA

PAMELA ELKIN
ASHEVILLE, NC

Our family loves this delicious strata at our Christmas morning breakfast! Wonderful served with fresh fruit. It's so simple...put it together the night before and chill overnight. In the morning, let it bake while you open your gifts. Enjoy!

Grease the bottom of a 13"x9" baking pan. Line bottom of pan with 6 slices bread; layer ham and cheese slices over bread. Top with remaining bread; set aside. Beat eggs in a large bowl. Whisk in milk and seasonings; pour over layers in pan. Cover pan with aluminum foil; chill for 8 hours or overnight. In the morning, remove foil; sprinkle with corn flake crumbs and drizzle with melted butter. Bake, uncovered, at 350 degrees for 1-1/2 hours, or until egg mixture is set.

Makes 8 servings.

12 slices white bread, divided
8 to 10 slices deli ham
8 to 10 slices Swiss or American cheese
7 eggs, beaten
4 c. milk
1 t. dry mustard
salt and pepper to taste
1 c. corn flake cereal, crushed, or more if desired
1/2 c. butter, melted

CHAPTER TWO

SOUTHERN-STYLE
Salads & Sides

TOSS TOGETHER GREAT TASTE AND HEALTHY GOODNESS TO MAKE FRESH, SATISFYING AND TASTY SALADS THAT ARE PACKED WITH FULL-ON FLAVOR.

PINEAPPLE CASSEROLE

LYNN FILIPOWICZ
WILMINGTON, NC

I have been making this dish for years...it's good hot or cold.

4 c. cold mashed
  potatoes
20-oz. can crushed
  pineapple
20-oz. can pineapple
  chunks, drained
2 c. shredded sharp
  Cheddar cheese
1/4 c. sugar
6 T. all-purpose flour
1 sleeve round buttery
  crackers, crushed
1/2 c. butter, melted
Optional: pineapple
  rings, maraschino
  cherries

Mix together all ingredients except crackers and butter in a greased 13"x9" baking pan. Top with crackers; drizzle butter over top. Bake, uncovered, at 350 degrees for about 30 minutes, or until heated through and bubbly. Garnish with pineapple rings and cherries, if desired.

Serves 8.

CHRIS'S SPICY MAC & CHEESE

CRYSTAL SHOOK
CATAWBA, NC

My son Chris loves this macaroni & cheese, and it's so simple!

16-oz. pkg. elbow
  macaroni, uncooked
15-oz. jar queso blanco
  dip

Cook pasta according to directions; drain and return to pan. Add dip to hot macaroni; stir and serve.

Makes 8 to 10 servings.

HAWAIIAN ASPARAGUS

BETH BROWN
TRENT WOODS, NC

This recipe was given to my mom forty years ago by another military wife when my Air Force family was stationed in Japan. We make this when asparagus is in season.

In a skillet over medium heat, cook asparagus in oil for 2 to 3 minutes. Add beef broth; cover, reduce heat and simmer for 4 to 5 minutes, until asparagus is cooked to desired tenderness. Stir in bacon, pepper and sesame seed.

Serves 4.

1 lb. asparagus, trimmed and cut in 1-inch diagonal slices

2 T. olive oil

1/4 c. beef broth

4 to 5 slices bacon, crisply cooked and cut into bite-size pieces

pepper to taste

2 T. sesame seed, lightly toasted

ZESTY WHITE BEAN SALAD

AMY THOMASON HUNT
TRAPHILL, NC

This tasty bean salad goes with anything! Try spooning it into toasted wonton cups for an easy appetizer too.

Combine all ingredients in a large serving bowl; toss to mix. Cover and refrigerate until serving time.

Makes 6 servings.

15-oz. can cannellini beans, drained and rinsed

1 tomato, diced

1/2 c. Kalamata olives, sliced

1/2 c. onion, diced

1/2 c. fresh basil, chopped

1 t. garlic, minced

1/3 c. sun-dried tomato vinaigrette salad dressing

salt and pepper to taste

MEXICAN LAYERED SALAD

**ANN CRANE
PLEASANT GARDEN, NC**

*This colorful salad is good to take to church functions or
reunions...it's always a hit! Serve it with a bowl of tortilla chips,
if you like.*

**4 c. romaine lettuce,
  torn**

**1 cucumber, peeled,
  halved and sliced**

3 tomatoes, chopped

**2 avocados, halved,
  pitted and sliced**

2 green peppers, chopped

1-1/2 c. mayonnaise

**1/2 c. chopped green
  chiles**

2 t. chili powder

1/2 t. onion powder

1/4 t. garlic powder

1/4 t. salt

**1 c. tortilla chips,
  crushed**

**1/2 c. shredded Cheddar
  cheese**

Optional: sour cream

In a 2-quart glass triffle or salad bowl, layer lettuce, cucumber, tomatoes, avocados and green peppers. Combine mayonnaise, chiles and seasonings; spread over top. Sprinkle with crushed chips and cheese. Top with sour cream, if desired. Serve immediately.

Makes 10 servings.

AUDREY'S CHICKEN & FRUIT SALAD

SHIRL PARSONS
CAPE CARTERET, NC

This was one of my mom's stand-by recipes. Mom would always make a big batch that would be gone in no time.

Combine chicken and celery in a large bowl; set aside. In a small bowl, combine mayonnaise and chili powder; add to chicken mixture and mix well. Cover and chill for 30 minutes. At serving time, add fruit and coconut; toss gently. To serve, spoon onto salad greens; sprinkle with peanuts. pepper and sesame seed.

Serves 6.

2 c. cooked chicken, cubed
1 c. celery, chopped
1 c. light mayonnaise
1/2 t. chili powder
20-oz. can pineapple chunks, drained
2 firm bananas, sliced
11-oz. can mandarin oranges, drained
1/2 c. flaked coconut
Garnish: salad greens, salted peanuts

HERB & CHEESE ORZO

LINDA KARNER
PISGAH FOREST, NC

Creamy and delicious...a great side dish for roast chicken or pork.

In a saucepan over medium heat, bring broth to a boil. Add butter and orzo; reduce heat and simmer until orzo absorbs broth, about 15 to 20 minutes. Stir in cheese, chives and pine nuts just before serving.

Makes 4 servings.

10-1/2 oz. can chicken broth
1 T. butter
1 c. orzo pasta, uncooked
1/2 c. shredded Asiago cheese
1/8 c. fresh chives, minced
1/4 c. pine nuts, toasted

GARLICKY SAVORY PARMESAN ASPARAGUS

JULIE VIDOVICH
WINSTON-SALEM, NC

*Savor the flavor of garden-fresh asparagus in this simple recipe...
nice with a baked ham.*

1 T. butter
1/4 c. olive oil
2 cloves garlic, minced
1 lb. asparagus spears, trimmed
2 t. lemon juice
salt and pepper to taste
Garnish: shredded Parmesan cheese

Combine butter and oil in a skillet over medium heat. Add garlic and sauté for one to 2 minutes. Add asparagus and cook to desired tenderness, stirring occasionally, about 10 minutes. Drain; sprinkle asparagus with lemon juice, salt and pepper. Arrange on serving platter; sprinkle with Parmesan cheese.

Makes 4 servings.

HERBED GARLIC BREAD

CHERYLANN SMITH
HILLSBOROUGH, NC

*A must-have with lasagna! Leftover slices make tasty salad
croutons...just cube and re-toast or fry them.*

1/2 c. butter, softened
1 sprig fresh rosemary
2 cloves garlic, pressed
1 t. Italian seasoning
1 t. dried basil
1 t. dried oregano
1 t. dried thyme
1 t. dried savory
1 t. dried marjoram
1 loaf country-style bread, sliced 1-inch thick

Combine butter and seasonings in a large microwave-safe mug. Microwave on high setting for one minute, until butter is melted; stir. Brush over both sides of bread slices; place bread on an ungreased baking sheet. Bake at 350 degrees until toasted, about 15 minutes.

Makes about 12 servings.

POTATO BISCUITS

SUSAN WILLIE
RIDGECREST, NC

These biscuits are wonderful with any meal.

In a bowl, mix all ingredients until a soft dough forms. Turn dough onto a surface lightly dusted with additional baking mix. Gently roll to coat. Shape into a ball; knead 3 or 4 times. Roll out dough 1/2-inch thick. Cut with a 2-inch biscuit cutter dipped in baking mix. Arrange on an ungreased baking sheet. Bake at 450 degrees for 10 to 12 minutes, until golden.

Makes 8 to 10 servings.

2-1/2 c. biscuit baking mix
1 c. mashed potatoes or sweet potatoes
1/3 c. margarine, softened
1/2 c. milk

CRANBERRY-APPLE BAKE

MACIE DILLING
RALEIGH, NC

Several years ago a good friend shared this side dish with me. Its sweet-tart flavor is perfect alongside savory turkey and dressing.

In a large bowl, combine apples, cranberries and 2 tablespoons flour. Toss to coat fruit. Add sugar, mixing well. Place in a lightly greased 2-quart casserole dish. In a medium bowl, combine oats, pecans, remaining flour and brown sugar. Blend in butter. Spoon oat mixture over fruit. Bake, uncovered, at 350 degrees for 45 minutes.

Makes 12 servings.

3 c. apples, cored, peeled and chopped
2 c. cranberries
1/2 c. plus 2 T. all-purpose flour, divided
1 c. sugar
3 1-5/8 oz. pkgs. instant cinnamon & spice oats
3/4 c. chopped pecans
1/2 c. brown sugar, packed
1/2 c. butter, melted

HARVEST BREAD

**AUDRA VANHORN-SOREY
COLUMBIA, NC**

*Be prepared to share this recipe! It's perfect for any potluck
dinner or get-together with family & friends.*

8-1/2 oz. pkg. corn
    muffin mix
2 eggs, beaten
1/4 c. butter, softened
1 c. shredded sharp
    Cheddar cheese
1 c. shredded Pepper
    Jack cheese
3/4 c. onion, diced
2-oz. jar diced pimentos
11-oz. can corn, drained
1 t. salt
Optional: 1 c. broccoli,
    finely chopped

In a bowl, combine dry muffin mix, eggs, butter
and cheeses. Mix well with a fork. Add remaining
ingredients; stir well. Pour batter into an ungreased
12"x9" baking pan. Bake at 375 degrees for 30
minutes, or until golden on top. Let stand for 30
minutes; cut into squares.

Makes 8 to 10 servings.

DINNERTIME CONVERSATION

The first outdoor drama in America, The
Lost Colony, is staged every year in Manteo,
entertaining thousands of visitors. This 84-year-
old musical under the stars tells the story of the
English settlers who arrived in 1587 and later
mysteriously disappeared. North Carolina native
Andy Griffith started his professional acting
career in the drama, working his way up to the
part of Sir Walter Raleigh.

CRAZY-GOOD POPOVERS

AMY THOMASON HUNT
TRAPHILL, NC

These little popovers are excellent with just about any meal you choose. They're even good as an appetizer or snack!

In a large bowl, combine all ingredients except butter. Mix thoroughly until a soft dough forms. Drop dough by tablespoonfuls onto a baking sheet sprayed with non-stick vegetable spray. Bake at 450 degrees for 7 to 9 minutes, until golden. Brush with melted butter; serve warm.

Makes about one dozen.

2 c. biscuit baking mix
2/3 c. milk
1/2 c. shredded Cheddar cheese
4 green onions, chopped
8 slices bacon, crisply cooked and crumbled
2 T. butter, melted

CREOLE CORNBREAD

CAROL CREEL
RALEIGH, NC

An instant family favorite!

Place frozen vegetables in a microwave-safe 10"x6" baking pan. Microwave on high setting for several minutes, until thawed. Stir in remaining ingredients except corn muffin mix; microwave until steaming. Prepare corn muffin mix according to package directions; spoon batter over hot vegetable mixture. Bake at 400 degrees for 25 to 30 minutes, until golden.

Serves 6.

10-oz. pkg. frozen mixed vegetables
8-oz. can tomato sauce
1 to 2 T. green pepper, chopped
1 green onion, sliced
1/8 t. salt
1/8 t. pepper
Optional: hot pepper sauce to taste
8-1/2 oz. pkg. corn muffin mix

CHEDDAR CHEESE BREAD

SHARMAN HESS
ASHEVILLE, NC

What a delicious bread served with soups and chili! This can be easily doubled for a 13"x9" pan. It's always a hit at bake sales.

1 egg, beaten
1/2 c. milk
1-1/2 c. biscuit baking mix
2 T. dried parsley
1 T. onion, minced
1-1/2 c. shredded Cheddar cheese, divided
1/4 c. butter, melted

In a bowl, whisk together egg and milk. Add biscuit mix, parsley, onion and 3/4 cup cheese to make a stiff batter. Spoon batter into a greased 8"x8" baking pan. Sprinkle with remaining cheese; drizzle with melted butter. Bake at 350 degrees for 25 minutes, or until golden.

Serves 4 to 6.

DIANE'S SKILLET CORNBREAD

DIANE GIRARD
ASHEBORO, NC

An elderly neighbor friend had been making this recipe for years, and got me to taste it...one taste and I was hooked! If you like a sweet, moist cornbread, you'll love this one.

1/2 c. margarine
2 8-1/2 oz. pkgs. corn muffin mix, divided
1/3 c. sugar
3 eggs, beaten
1/2 c. milk
Garnish: additional melted margarine

Place margarine in a cast-iron skillet; melt in a 350-degree oven. Place 1-1/2 packages muffin mix in a large bowl, reserving remaining mix for another recipe. Stir in sugar, eggs and milk; mix well and pour in melted margarine from skillet. Stir; pour batter into skillet. Bake at 350 degrees for 30 minutes, or until light golden. Brush top with margarine; cut into wedges and serve hot.

Serves 8.

RANCH VEGETABLE BUNDLES

PATTI WALKER
MOCKSVILLE, NC

I like to make vegetable packets to go along with any main dish I'm serving. They are so easy and I can add meat to them if I want an all-in-one meal. You can also make individual bundles with the vegetables that each family member likes best.

Place potatoes in the middle of a piece of aluminum foil. Layer zucchini, squash and carrots over potatoes. Add onion; season with garlic salt and pepper to taste. Sprinkle on dressing mix and dot with butter. Fold up ends of aluminum foil over vegetables; secure tightly. Place on a baking sheet and bake at 375 degrees for 30 to 35 minutes. Remove bundles from oven; carefully cut an opening in foil to vent steam before serving.

Makes 6 to 8 servings.

4 potatoes, peeled and sliced
2 zucchini, sliced
2 yellow squash, sliced
8 baby carrots, grated
1 onion, sliced
garlic salt and pepper to taste
1-oz. pkg. ranch salad dressing mix
3 T. butter, diced

CRANBERRY-APPLE SALAD

SUSAN WILLIE
RIDGECREST, NC

This recipe is quick & easy. Very tasty and festive!

In a salad bowl, mix cranberry sauce, celery and apple. Cover and refrigerate. Stir in walnuts just before serving.

Makes 6 servings.

2 c. whole-berry cranberry sauce
1 green apple, cored and diced
1 stalk celery, finely chopped
1/2 c. chopped walnuts

MEXICAN SLAW

**ASHLEY JONES
GATES, NC**

This recipe was handed down to my mom by her mom. We make it every Sunday and the bowl gets filled up three times...it goes fast. It's such a good Sunday dish! Enjoy as a side salad, as an appetizer with tortilla chips or spooned over a Mexican-style main dish.

1 head cabbage, shredded

1 c. grape tomatoes, sliced

1/2 c. white onion, coarsely chopped

1/2 c. red onion, coarsely chopped

2 green onions, finely chopped

2 bunches fresh cilantro, coarsely chopped

2 4-oz. cans chopped jalapeño peppers

1/4 c. olive oil

3 T. rice vinegar

1 t. garlic powder

2 t. ground cumin

salt and pepper to taste

Toss together fresh vegetables and cilantro in a large bowl. Add jalapeños with juice and remaining ingredients; toss again. Let stand 30 minutes before serving.

Makes 12 to 14 servings.

KITCHEN TIP

A few drops of lemon juice in the water will whiten boiled potatoes.

2-4-1 DROP BISCUITS

CRYSTAL SHOOK
CATAWBA, NC

These are so simple! Serve warm with butter and jam.

Combine all ingredients in a large bowl; mix well. Drop dough by tablespoonfuls onto a greased baking sheet. Bake at 350 degrees for 20 to 25 minutes, until golden.

2 c. self-rising flour
1 c. milk
1/4 c. shortening

Makes one dozen.

COWGIRL UP & CORNBREAD

JENNIFER RUBINO
HICKORY, NC

What do you do when everyone's hungry and you're out of time? Cowgirl up! This tasty chow is ready in less than 30 minutes.

Prepare and bake cornbread according to package directions. Meanwhile, brown beef and onion in a skillet over medium heat; drain. Add beans and corn to beef mixture; heat through. Serve beef mixture over squares of warm cornbread.

8-1/2 oz. pkg. corn muffin mix
1 to 1-1/2 lbs. lean ground beef
1/2 onion, diced
22-oz. can smoky baked beans
11-oz. can corn, drained

Serves 4.

AMY'S 2-SQUASH DELIGHT

AMY JONES
GRAHAM, NC

After we started harvesting our first garden, I came up with this recipe...
it's so delicious, it's a new summer tradition!

1 yellow squash, diced
1 zucchini, diced
14-1/2 oz. can fire-
  roasted diced tomatoes
2 T. extra-virgin olive
  oil
1 t. Italian seasoning
Garnish: grated
  Parmesan cheese

In a skillet, combine squash, zucchini, undrained tomatoes, oil and seasoning. Simmer over medium heat until squash is tender. Top with Parmesan cheese before serving.

Makes 4 servings.

ZESTY BLACK-EYED PEAS

ANGELA BISSETTE
MIDDLESEX, NC

This simple recipe is excellent served with pork and also can
be served over rice. For a less spicy version, just substitute an
undrained can of stewed tomatoes for the tomatoes with chiles.

1/2 c. onion, diced
2 T. garlic, minced
1 T. oil
2 15-oz cans black-eyed
  peas
10-oz. can diced
  tomatoes with green
  chiles

In a skillet over medium heat, sauté onion and garlic in oil for 5 minutes. Stir in undrained peas and tomatoes. Reduce heat to low; simmer for 15 to 20 minutes.

Serves 6.

NOT YOUR GRANNY'S BRUSSELS SPROUTS

LYNNETTE JONES
EAST FLAT ROCK, NC

Remember those soggy boiled Brussels sprouts Grandma used to serve? No more, with this updated recipe!

In a skillet over medium heat, cook bacon until crisp. Set bacon aside, reserving one teaspoon drippings. In a large bowl, toss Brussels sprouts with reserved drippings, olive oil and salt. Arrange sprouts on a lightly greased baking sheet. Bake, uncovered, at 350 degrees for 15 to 20 minutes, until just tender. Turn oven to broil. Broil sprouts for 2 to 3 minutes, just until slightly charred. Meanwhile, combine syrup, vinegar and spice in a small saucepan; simmer over low heat for several minutes. Toss sprouts with syrup mixture and reserved bacon.

Makes 6 to 8 servings.

2 slices bacon, diced
2 lbs. Brussels sprouts, trimmed and halved or quartered
1 T. olive oil
1 t. salt
2 T. pure maple syrup
1 t. cider vinegar
1 t. Chinese 5-spice powder, or 1/8 t. cinnamon plus 1/8 t. pepper

SKILLET POTATO PIE

SHIRL PARSONS
CAPE CARTERET, NC

Looks like lots more effort than it is!

Slice potatoes 1/4-inch thick. Place in a bowl; mash lightly just until broken up. Stir in buttermilk and green onions; season with salt and pepper. In a non-stick skillet over medium heat, heat just enough oil to coat skillet. Spoon potato mixture into skillet; pat evenly. Cook until potatoes are crisp and golden on the bottom. Slide out onto a plate and cut into wedges.

Serves 4.

1-1/2 lbs. redskin potatoes, boiled
1/2 c. buttermilk
2 green onions, minced
salt and pepper to taste
oil for frying

WHEAT BERRY & WILD RICE SALAD

LINDA KARNER
PISGAH FOREST, NC

This is a recipe I made up myself, and my family loves it! You can add any fresh herbs that you like. Be sure to allow enough time for the wheat berries to soak.

1 c. wheat berries, uncooked

1 c. wild rice, uncooked

1 red or green pepper, diced

1 red onion, chopped

1/2 c. walnuts, toasted and coarsely chopped

1/4 c. fresh oregano, chopped

4 to 5 leaves fresh basil, chopped

3 sprigs fresh parsley, chopped

vinaigrette salad dressing to taste

Cover wheat berries with water in a saucepan; soak for 8 hours to overnight. The next day, drain wheat berries well; add fresh cold water to cover. Cook over medium heat for about one hour, until tender; drain well. Meanwhile, in a separate saucepan, cover rice with cold water. Cook for about 30 minutes, until tender; drain well. Combine wheat berries and rice in a serving bowl. Add remaining ingredients, adding salad dressing to taste. For the best flavor, serve at room temperature; may also be served chilled.

Serves 6 to 8.

JUST FOR FUN

In the 1920s, a road-building effort was begun to connect all the county seats in the state with hard-surfaced roads. This led to North Carolina being known as the "Good Roads State."

PUMPKIN-CARAMEL DOUGHNUT HOLES

AMY BRADSHER
ROXBORO, NC

One day, my daughter and I experimented with some pumpkin and came up with these yummy doughnut holes. We love the gooey sweetness of the caramel glaze on top...my husband says that they're perfect fresh from the oven!

In a bowl, mix together flour, cinnamon, baking powder, baking soda and salt; set aside. In a separate large bowl, beat together butter and brown sugar. Mix in egg, pumpkin, milk and sour cream. Slowly mix flour mixture into egg mixture until just combined; add chocolate chips, if using. Batter will be thick. Lightly grease a mini muffin tin. Add a tablespoon of batter to each mini muffin cup. Bake at 325 degrees for 10 to 15 minutes, until a toothpick tests clean. Cool in pan for 2 to 3 minutes. Remove from pan and cool completely. Dip doughnut holes into Caramel Glaze before serving.

Caramel Glaze:

In a bowl, stir together all ingredients.

Serves 6.

2 c. white whole-wheat flour
2 t. cinnamon
1-1/2 t. baking powder
1-1/2 t. baking soda
1/2 t. salt
1/4 c. butter, softened
1/3 c. brown sugar, packed
1 egg, beaten
15-oz. can pumpkin
1/3 to 1/2 c. milk
3/4 c. sour cream
Optional: 1/2 c. chocolate chips

CARAMEL GLAZE
1 c. powdered sugar
2 T. milk
1 to 2 T. caramel ice cream topping

SLOW-COOKER BEANS

DARCY ANDERS
HENDERSONVILLE, NC

Tossing everything in the slow cooker means more time with the family!

1 lb. ground beef

1 onion, chopped

4 to 6 slices bacon, crisply cooked and crumbled

2 T. oil

1 c. catsup

1 T. Worcestershire sauce

1 t. cider vinegar

1 t. mustard

1 t. salt

1/3 c. brown sugar, packed

2 16-oz. cans pork & beans

Brown beef and onion; set aside. Mix together bacon, oil, catsup, Worcestershire sauce, vinegar, mustard, salt and brown sugar; add to beef. Stir in beans. Pour mixture into a slow cooker. Cover and cook on high setting for one hour, or until heated through.

Serves 6 to 8.

BEER BREAD BISCUITS

MERTIE STARDEVANT
WASHINGTON, NC

This simple recipe is from my sister-in-law. It's a hit every time we have soup!

2 c. biscuit baking mix

12-oz. can regular or non-alcoholic beer

3 T. sugar

Combine all ingredients in a bowl; mix well. Spoon batter into greased muffin cups, filling 3/4 full. Bake at 325 degrees for 20 minutes.

Makes 6 to 8 biscuits.

HARVEST PUMPKIN-APPLE BREAD

**SHARMAN HESS
ASHEVILLE, NC**

Truly a comforting treat with the pumpkin and apple flavors together. An extremely moist, delicious bread. The recipe makes 2 loaves...great for bake sales or sharing with friends and neighbors.

In a large bowl, combine flour, baking soda, salt and cinnamon; mix well. In another bowl, combine pumpkin, sugar, eggs, oil and apple juice; stir until just blended. Add pumpkin mixture to flour mixture; stir until moistened. Fold in apple. Spoon batter evenly into 2 greased 9"x5" loaf pans. Bake at 350 degrees for 65 to 70 minutes. Cool in pans on a wire rack; turn out and finish cooling.

Makes 2 loaves.

3 c. all-purpose flour
2 t. baking soda
1-1/2 t. salt
2 t. cinnamon
15-oz. can pumpkin
3 c. sugar
4 eggs, lightly beaten
1 c. canola oil
1/2 c. apple juice
1 baking apple, peeled, cored and diced

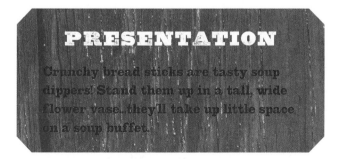

PRESENTATION

Crunchy bread sticks are tasty soup dippers! Stand them up in a tall, wide flower vase...they'll take up little space on a soup buffet.

CRUNCHY CASHEW SLAW

LORI COMER
KERNERSVILLE, NC

A dear friend brought this salad to our Sunday School dinner after church...every lady there wanted the recipe! It's scrumptious and so simple to make.

16-oz. pkg. coleslaw mix
2 3-oz. pkgs. chicken-flavored ramen noodles
1/2 c. sugar
1/3 c. vinegar
1/4 c. oil
1 c. cashew halves
1 c. sunflower seeds

Place coleslaw mix in a large salad bowl. Crush noodles and add to coleslaw, setting aside seasoning packets; toss to mix. In a separate small bowl, whisk together sugar, vinegar, oil and reserved seasoning; pour over coleslaw mixture. Toss again; cover and chill 2 hours. Do not chill overnight as the noodles will become soggy. At serving time, add cashew halves and sunflower seeds. Mix well and serve.

Makes 10 to 12 servings.

CARROT CAKE MUFFINS

BECKY DANIELSON
HAYESVILLE, NC

My kids love these quick and nutritious muffins. They're a great treat after supper with a glass of milk. For a richer treat, substitute devil's food cake mix for the carrot cake mix.

15-1/4 oz. pkg. carrot cake mix
15-oz. can pumpkin

Add dry cake mix to a large bowl. Add pumpkin; stir until well mixed. Line a muffin tin with paper liners; spray with non-stick vegetable spray. Spoon batter into 18 muffin cups, filling 2/3 full. Bake at 350 degrees for 14 to 18 minutes, until muffins test done with a toothpick. Remove to a wire rack; cool.

Makes 1-1/2 dozen.

BROCCOLI-CORN CASSEROLE

DENISE HENNEBURY
GREENSBORO, NC

In 1976, my husband and I were alone for Thanksgiving in Vermont. We lived in the lower level of an old farmhouse, and our upstairs neighbors, another young couple who were alone for the holiday, invited us for dinner. Our hostess served this wonderful side dish, and she was kind enough to share the recipe with me. I have made this delicious casserole dozens of times since then... I have yet to find someone who doesn't love it!

Cook or microwave broccoli for about one minute; break apart. In a bowl, mix broccoli and remaining ingredients except butter and stuffing mix; set aside. Melt butter in a saucepan over low heat. Add stuffing mix; toss to mix and remove from heat immediately. Stir one cup stuffing mixture into broccoli mixture. Turn into an ungreased 1-1/2 quart casserole dish; sprinkle with remaining stuffing mixture. Bake, uncovered, at 350 degrees for 35 to 40 minutes, until top is golden.

Serves 4 to 6.

10-oz. pkg. frozen chopped broccoli
16-oz. can cream-style corn
1 egg, lightly beaten
1 T. onion, minced
1/4 t. salt
1/8 t. pepper
3 T. butter
1-2/3 c. herb-seasoned stuffing mix, divided

CHAPTER THREE

RACEWAY

Soups & Sandwiches

BEACH-SIDE OR 'ROUND THE
CAMPFIRE TOGETHER, COZY UP
WITH A BOWL OF HEARTY SOUP OR
A TASTY SANDWICH PERFECT FOR
PACKN' IN THE PICNIC BASKET!

PULLED PORK BARBECUE

MELANIE FOSTER
NORTH WILKESBORO, NC

This is a budget-friendly, family-pleasing main dish that is requested often in my home. Great served with a side of slaw and baked beans.

14-oz. can beef broth

1/2 c. regular or non-alcoholic beer

3 to 4-lb. Boston butt pork roast

18-oz. bottle smoke-flavored barbecue sauce

sandwich buns, split

Pour broth and beer into a large slow cooker; add roast. Cover and cook on high setting for 4 hours, or on low setting for 8 hours, until roast is very tender. Remove roast from slow cooker. Shred roast with 2 forks and transfer to a roasting pan. Stir in barbecue sauce. Bake, uncovered, at 350 degrees for 30 minutes. Fill buns with pulled pork to make sandwiches.

Makes 10 to 12 servings.

SMOKED SAUSAGE-WHITE BEAN SOUP

ANGELA BISSETTE
MIDDLESEX, NC

My husband loves soup, so I created this one for him. It is so simple to prepare and tastes great with a slice of warm homemade bread.

14-oz. pkg. smoked pork sausage, sliced

2 T. oil

1 green pepper, diced

1 onion, diced

2 T. garlic, minced

14-1/2 oz. can diced tomatoes

2 15-oz. cans Great Northern beans, drained and rinsed

2 14-1/2 oz. cans chicken broth

In a soup pot over medium heat, brown sausage in oil for 5 minutes. Drain; add green pepper, onion and garlic. Cook for 10 minutes. Stir in tomatoes with juice, beans and chicken broth; bring to a boil. Reduce heat to low; simmer for 30 minutes.

Makes 8 servings.

GAME-DAY SANDWICH

**YVONNE COLEMAN
STATESVILLE, NC**

*My husband loves this sandwich and requests it on his birthday. It
has something to please everyone.*

Mix mayonnaise and mustard together. Cut bread
horizontally into 3 layers. Spread half of mayonnaise
mixture on the bottom layer. Add turkey, roast beef,
Swiss cheese and lettuce. Cover with middle bread
layer; spread with remaining mayonnaise mixture.
Add ham, bacon, Cheddar cheese and tomato. Top
with remaining bread layer. Cut into 6 to 8 slices.

Makes 6 to 8 servings.

3 T. mayonnaise

1 T. mustard

1-lb. round loaf
Hawaiian-style bread

1/4 lb. sliced deli turkey

1/4 lb. sliced deli roast
beef

3 slices Swiss cheese

3 lettuce leaves

1/4 lb. sliced deli ham

6 slices bacon, crisply
cooked

3 slices Cheddar cheese

6 slices tomato

DADDY'S CORNED BEEF SOUP

BONNIE ROGERS
GOLDSHORE, NC

My dad made up this soup recipe one night, when he needed to feed a hungry child. It can be made in no time if you need a quick meal.

12-oz. can corned beef, broken up
1 onion, diced
14-1/2 oz. can diced tomatoes
14-3/4 oz. can creamed corn
14-1/2 oz. can baby lima beans
salt and pepper to taste
Optional: shredded Cheddar cheese

In a large saucepan, combine all ingredients except optional cheese; do not drain tomatoes. Cook over medium heat until heated through and onion is tender. Serve topped with cheese, if desired.

Makes 4 to 6 servings.

CREAMY CHICKEN CHILI

ANGELA BISSETTE
MIDDLESEX, NC

This recipe is both delicious and easy to prepare. Add a crisp tossed salad and homemade crusty bread for a complete meal.

4 boneless chicken thighs, cooked and diced
2 15-oz. cans Great Northern beans
10-3/4 oz. can cream of chicken soup
32-oz. container chicken broth
10-oz. can diced tomatoes with green chiles
Garnish: shredded Cheddar cheese, sour cream

In a large soup pot, combine chicken, undrained beans, soup, broth and tomatoes. Bring to a boil over medium-high heat. Reduce heat to medium-low. Simmer, stirring occasionally, for 30 to 45 minutes. Garnish individual servings as desired.

Makes 8 servings.

SPICY CORN CHOWDER WITH COUNTRY SIDE MEAT

PASTOR JEFF BROWN
ICARD, NC

I'm a pastor from North Carolina. Cooking is my stress reliever after a long day of ministry. I created this rich-tasting chowder several years ago in trial & error fashion and have made it for my congregation. Some of my church members frequently ask me to make it for them! Serve with buttery crackers or fresh bread.

In a stew pot over medium-high heat, cover potatoes with water. Boil until just tender, but still firm. Drain well, discarding water; return potatoes to pot and set aside. Meanwhile, in a skillet over low heat, melt butter with oil. Sauté onions and celery, sprinkling well with salt. Sprinkle flour over onion mixture; cook and stir for one to 2 minutes. Add onion mixture, corn and half-and-half or milk to potatoes in stew pot. Bring to a boil, stirring often. Simmer chowder over low heat to desired thickness, adding a little more half-and-half or milk if too thick. Season with more salt, if needed. Add cayenne pepper to taste, if desired. While chowder is simmering, cook side meat or bacon in a skillet over medium heat until crisp. Top each bowlful with small pieces of crisp side meat or bacon.

Makes 6 to 8 servings.

4 to 6 waxy potatoes, peeled and diced

2 T. butter, sliced

2 T. olive oil

1 to 2 onions, diced

3 stalks celery, diced

salt to taste

3 to 4 T. all-purpose flour

2 to 3 c. frozen shoepeg corn

8 c. half-and-half or whole milk

Optional: cayenne pepper to taste

Optional: 1/3 c. fresh parsley, chopped

1/2 lb. pork side meat or thick country bacon, diced

ALMOST NORTH CAROLINA PULLED PORK BBQ

JOAN OSBORNE
BOOMER, NC

My family often requests this recipe. We serve ours on buns southern-style, topped with coleslaw and extra hot sauce. Some of us like to also add sliced sweet onion and tomato, mustard, pickled jalapeños and dill pickle chips. Occasionally we have a guest who also likes mayonnaise on theirs. However you enjoy it, it's delicious!

4 to 5-lb. Boston butt pork roast
salt and pepper to taste
1/3 c. cider vinegar
1 to 2 T. molasses
several drops smoke-flavored cooking sauce
1 onion, diced
1 T. olive oil or butter
1/4 c. tomato sauce or catsup
18-oz. bottle barbecue sauce
several drops hot pepper sauce
15 hamburger buns, split
Garnish: favorite sandwich toppings

Season roast with salt and pepper; place in a 6-quart slow cooker. Drizzle with vinegar, molasses and smoke-flavored sauce, as desired. Cover and cook on low setting for about 10 hours. Remove roast to a plate; cool, discarding bones and fat. Return roast to slow cooker; pull apart with 2 forks. In a skillet over medium heat, sauté onion in oil or butter. Add onion to slow cooker along with tomato sauce or catsup, barbecue sauce and hot sauce. Turn slow cooker to warm until serving time, stirring occasionally to blend flavors. Spoon onto buns; add toppings as desired.

Makes 15 or more sandwiches.

YUMMY SLOPPY JOES

MONICA PEDELTY SIMPSON
BURLINGTON, NC

This is a recipe from a child's cookbook that was given to me by my grandparents when I was eight years old. My mom and I added a few ingredients to suit our family's taste. My husband, who does not care for ground beef, loves these sandwiches! It is a quick & easy weekday fix.

Brown beef in a deep skillet over medium heat; drain. Stir in remaining ingredients except buns. Simmer for about 5 to 10 minutes, stirring occasionally, until sauce is slightly thickened. Spoon onto buns and serve.

Makes 6 to 8 sandwiches.

1 lb. ground beef
1 c. catsup
3 T. brown sugar, packed
2 T. mustard
2 T. cider vinegar
1/2 t. garlic powder
1/2 t. onion salt
1 t. Worcestershire sauce
6 to 8 hamburger buns, split

JUST FOR FUN
The first known miniature golf course was in Fayetteville, North Carolina.

CAROLINA GARDEN STEW

**TABETHA STONE
EASTOVER, NC**

*A woman whom I knew for 20 years gave me this delicious recipe.
She taught me so many wonderful recipes. She was our local
colorful character and a wonderfully sweet woman.*

**2 qts. beef broth or
water**

**2 to 3 lbs. stew beef
cubes**

**3 to 4 potatoes, peeled
and cubed**

2 onions, cubed

**4 carrots, peeled &
sliced 1/2-inch thick**

**2 to 3 stalks celery,
sliced 1/2-inch thick**

**1 green, yellow or red
pepper, cubed**

2 t. dried parsley

1 t. onion powder

1 t. paprika

salt to taste

1 t. pepper

2 T. cornstarch

Place broth or water in a large stockpot over medium-high heat. Add remaining ingredients except cornstarch; bring to a boil. Reduce heat to a simmer; cover and cook for about 1-1/2 hours. Shortly before serving, place cornstarch in a small bowl. Add 1/4 cup cooking liquid; mix well. Stir back into simmering stew; continue cooking for several minutes, until thickened.

Makes 4 to 6 servings.

SOUTHWESTERN SOUP

**KIMBERLY BAGLEY
MORRISVILLE, NC**

All four of my children love this soup. I even make it for my church's weekly dinners. It is really simple and quick to put together. I have tried it with leftover shredded chicken and with ground turkey too. Try it and you'll agree it's delicious!

Heat oil in a soup pot over medium heat; sauté onion and garlic. Add beef and cook until browned; drain and stir in seasoning mix. Add tomatoes with juice, corn, beans and broth. Stir well; simmer for 10 minutes. Serve with your favorite toppings.

Makes 6 servings.

1 T. oil

1/2 c. onion, chopped

4 cloves garlic, chopped

1 lb. ground beef

1-oz. pkg. chipotle taco seasoning mix

28-oz. can diced tomatoes with green chiles

2 c. frozen corn

2 15-oz. cans black beans, drained

2 28-oz. containers beef broth

Garnish: shredded Mexican-Blend cheese, sour cream, salsa, sliced avocado, chopped fresh cilantro, tortilla chips

BEEFY MACARONI SOUP

SHARON TRAX
KERNERSVILLE, NC

*We all love this hearty soup! Just add a basket of crusty rolls for
a yummy cool-weather meal.*

1 lb. stew beef cubes
1 t. garlic powder
1/2 t. pepper
2 T. oil
4 c. water
15-oz. can diced
  tomatoes
1/2 cup elbow macaroni,
  uncooked
1.35-oz. pkg. onion soup
  mix
16-oz. pkg. frozen mixed
  vegetables, thawed

Sprinkle beef with garlic powder and pepper. In a
Dutch oven over medium-high heat, brown beef
in oil; drain. Add water and tomatoes with juice;
simmer for 30 minutes, or until beef is tender. Stir in
uncooked macaroni and soup mix; return to a boil.
Add vegetables. Reduce heat; cover and simmer
for 10 minutes, stirring occasionally, until beef and
macaroni are tender.

Makes 4 to 6 servings.

EASY TACO SOUP

AUDRA VANHORN-SOREY
COLUMBIA, NC

*This is a simple slow-cooker twist on taco soup...and with just six
ingredients! Garnish bowls of soup with all your favorite toppings
like shredded cheese, sour cream and green onions. Yum!*

1 lb. lean ground beef
1-1/4 oz. pkg. taco
  seasoning mix
15-1/2 oz. can kidney
  beans
15-1/2 oz. can black
  beans
15-1/4 oz. can corn
14-1/2 oz. can diced
  tomatoes

Brown beef in a skillet over medium heat; drain and
stir in seasoning mix. Transfer beef to a 5-quart slow
cooker. Add remaining ingredients; do not drain any
of the cans. Stir. Cover and cook on low setting for 4
to 6 hours, stirring occasionally.

Makes 8 servings.

MEDITERRANEAN SANDWICHES

SHIRL PARSONS
CAPE CARTERET, NC

This is a tasty twist on the "usual" chicken salad sandwich.

Combine chicken, basil, salt and pepper in a stockpot. Cover with water and bring to a boil. Reduce heat and simmer, covered, 10 to 12 minutes until chicken is no longer pink in center. Remove chicken from pan; set aside to cool. Cube chicken and combine with remaining ingredients except rolls and garnish. Toss well to coat. Spread rolls with additional mayonnaise; top with lettuce and chicken salad mixture.

Makes 6 servings.

4 boneless, skinless chicken breasts
1 t. dried basil
1/4 t. salt
1/4 t. pepper
1 c. cucumber, chopped
1/2 c. mayonnaise
1/4 c. roasted red pepper, chopped
1/4 c. sliced black olives
1/4 c. plain yogurt
1/4 t. garlic powder
6 kaiser rolls, split
Garnish: mayonnaise, lettuce leaves

DINNERTIME CONVERSATION

In western North Carolina, a natural wonder called the Blowing Rock has been a tourist destination since 1933. The town of Blowing Rock takes its name from an unusual rock formation which juts over 1,500 feet above the Johns River gorge. Wind currents from the gorge often blow vertically, causing light objects to float upwards into the sky.

ALBERTA PRAIRIE BURGERS

**SHIRL PARSONS
CAPE CARTERET, NC**

*This is a wonderful savory burger from my home of Alberta, Canada.
What sets this burger apart from others is the sour cream in the beef
mixture, which gives it lots of flavor and juiciness.*

1 lb. ground beef

1/2 c. quick-cooking oats,
uncooked

1/4 c. light sour cream

1/4 c. mushrooms,
minced

1 onion, finely chopped

3 cloves garlic, minced

1 T. Dijon mustard

1 T. fresh parsley,
chopped

1 t. dried oregano

1 t. dried thyme

1/4 t. salt

1/4 t. pepper

4 to 6 hamburger buns,
split

Combine all ingredients except buns; mix lightly,
blending well. Form into 4 to 6 burgers, one to 2
inches thick. Grill on a lightly oiled grill over medium
heat for 5 to 7 minutes per side, turning once, to
desired doneness. May broil or pan-fry if preferred.
Serve on buns.

Makes 4 to 6 sandwiches.

PRESENTATION

Float whole strawberries and lime
slices in your iced herbal tea, pretty!

SANTA FE SOUP

**KAY JOHNSON
WASHINGTON, NC**

This soup is always very popular when I take it to church dinners or fundraising events. A friend shared a similar recipe with me that called for ground beef. I substituted ground turkey and you cannot tell the difference.

In a stockpot over medium heat, brown turkey or beef and onion; drain. Stir in dressing mix and water. Add corn, beans and tomatoes; do not drain cans. Bring to a boil; reduce heat to low. Simmer for 2 hours, stirring occasionally. Add a little water if soup gets too thick. Serve with tortilla chips, garnished with desired toppings.

Makes 15 to 20 servings.

2 lbs. ground turkey or beef

1 onion, chopped

2-oz. pkg. ranch salad dressing mix

2 c. water

2 15-oz. cans white shoepeg corn

15-1/2 oz. can black beans

15-1/2 oz. can kidney beans

15-1/2 oz. can pinto beans

14-1/2 oz. can diced tomatoes with green chiles

14-1/2 oz. can tomato wedges or diced tomatoes

tortilla chips

Garnish: sour cream, shredded Cheddar cheese, sliced green onions

FIESTA CORN CHOWDER

**SANDRA TURNER
FAYETTEVILLE, NC**

The first time I made this soup was for a progressive dinner when my home was the "soup & salad" stop. It has become a family favorite whenever we have Mexican meals. I keep the ingredients on hand, and it only takes a few minutes to make this soup.

14-3/4 oz. can creamed corn
14-1/2 oz. can chicken broth
2 10-oz. cans diced tomatoes with green chiles
11-oz. can sweet corn & diced peppers, drained
1 lb. pasteurized process cheese, cubed

In a soup pot, combine all ingredients. Bring to a boil over medium-high heat, stirring frequently. Reduce heat to medium-low. Cover and simmer for 4 to 5 minutes, until cheese is melted and soup is heated through.

Makes 6 servings.

DINNERTIME CONVERSATION

The Tweetsie Railroad is a popular tourist attraction between Boone and Blowing Rock. It's pulled by a coal-fired steam locomotive, the only surviving narrow-gauge engine of the East Tennessee and Western North Carolina Railroad (ET&WNC). Area residents fondly called it "Tweetsie," suggested by the initials and also by the shrill "tweet, tweet" of the train whistle. In 2017, Locomotive #12 celebrated its 100th birthday.

EGG SALAD SANDWICHES

CHERYLANN SMITH
HILLSBOROUGH, NC

Some days, there's nothing better than an old-fashioned egg salad sandwich and a cup of soup! Adjust the mayonnaise and mustard amounts to suit your family's taste.

Mix together eggs, mayonnaise, mustard, salt and pepper until well blended. Sprinkle with paprika. Spoon onto half of bread slices. Top with tomato slices and remaining bread slices.

Makes 10 to 12 servings.

1 doz. eggs, hard-boiled,
  peeled and chopped
1/2 c. mayonnaise
2 T. Dijon mustard
salt and pepper to taste
paprika to taste
1 loaf sliced whole-
  wheat bread, divided
Garnish: tomato slices

TURKEY BLT ROLL-UPS

JEWEL SHARPE
RALEIGH, NC

Yum...who wouldn't love these hearty, satisfying roll-ups?

In a small bowl, mix cream cheese and mayonnaise; stir in bacon. Spread cream cheese mixture over each tortilla. Top with turkey, tomatoes and lettuce; roll tortillas up tightly. Serve immediately, or wrap in plastic wrap and refrigerate up to 24 hours.

Serves 4.

1/4 c. chive & onion
  cream cheese spread
2 T. mayonnaise
8 slices bacon, diced and
  crisply cooked
4 8-inch flour tortillas
6-oz. pkg. thinly sliced
  deli turkey
1 c. roma tomatoes,
  chopped
1 c. lettuce, shredded

HEARTY FISH CHOWDER

MIA ROSSI
CHARLOTTE, NC

This savory chowder was one of the seven fish dishes my family shared on Christmas Eve. It's delicious anytime, though!

2 T. olive oil
1/2 c. sweet onion, chopped
3 c. celery, chopped
2 carrots, peeled and grated
1 to 2 potatoes, peeled and diced
1 to 2 leeks, chopped
1 clove garlic, minced
14-oz. can chicken broth
1-1/2 c. water
1 t. seafood seasoning
1-1/2 t. salt
1/2 t. pepper
1 lb. grouper or tilapia fillets, cut into large cubes
1 c. half-and-half
Garnish: butter, oyster crackers

Heat oil in a soup pot over medium heat. Sauté onion for 5 minutes, or until tender. Add celery, carrots, potatoes, leeks and garlic. Cook for 7 minutes, stirring occasionally. Add broth, water and seasonings; bring to a boil. Reduce heat to medium-low; cover and simmer for 30 minutes. Add fish; cover and simmer for 20 minutes. Stir in half-and-half; heat through but do not boil. Top each bowl with a pat of butter; serve with oyster crackers.

Makes 8 servings.

BEEF EYE ROAST FOR SANDWICHES

KRISTIE BOULDIN
TRINITY, NC

This recipe is so delicious, we fell in love with it many years ago. It's so easy to do...great for get-togethers and parties any time!

Sprinkle roast lightly all over with flour; set aside. In a large Dutch oven with a lid, melt shortening over medium-high heat. Add roast; brown on all sides. In a bowl, mix together remaining ingredients except buns and coleslaw; spoon over roast. Cover and bake at 325 degrees for 2-3/4 hours, or until very tender. The pan juices will become a delicious gravy as the roast cooks. Shred roast with 2 forks; stir into juices. Serve beef on buns, topped with coleslaw if desired.

Makes 8 to 10 sandwiches.

3 to 4-lb. beef eye roast
2 T. all-purpose flour
2 T. shortening
1/2 c. pineapple juice
1.05-oz. pkg. Italian salad dressing mix
1 T. dried, minced onion
1 T. lemon juice
1 T. Worcestershire sauce
2 T. salt
1/8 t. pepper
8 to 10 sandwich buns, split
Optional: coleslaw

CHEESY BURGER SOUP

CRYSTAL SHOOK
CATAWBA, NC

One of my son's favorite comfort foods. Great served in homemade bread bowls!

1 lb. ground beef
4 T. butter, divided
3/4 c. onion, chopped
3/4 c. carrots, peeled and shredded
3/4 c. celery, diced
1 t. dried basil
1. t. dried parsley
3 c. chicken broth
4 c. potatoes, peeled and diced
1/4 c. all-purpose flour
8-oz. pkg. pasteurized process cheese, cubed
1-1/2 c. milk
3/4 t. salt
1/4 t. pepper
1/4 c. sour cream

Brown beef in a skillet over medium heat; drain and set aside. Meanwhile, in a soup pot, melt one tablespoon butter over medium heat. Sauté onion, carrots, celery, basil and parsley until vegetables are tender. Add broth, potatoes and beef; bring to a boil. Reduce heat to medium-low and simmer for 10 to 12 minutes, until potatoes are tender. Melt remaining butter in a small skillet over medium heat; sprinkle with flour. Cook, stirring often, for 3 to 5 minutes, until bubbly. Add to soup; bring to a boil. Cook and stir for 2 minutes. Reduce heat to low. Add cheese, milk and seasonings; cook until cheese melts. Blend in sour cream.

Makes 8 servings.

"MOM, IT'S GOOD" CHILI

MARY BAKER
FOUNTAIN, NC

My two picky teenagers seldom comment on anything I cook...but this chili was a real winner!

In a stockpot, brown beef over medium heat; drain. Add other ingredients except water and cheese. Reduce heat to low; cover and simmer for 3 hours, stirring occasionally. If needed, add water to desired thickness. Serve topped with cheese.

Makes 12 servings.

2 lbs. ground beef

2 onions, chopped

2 green peppers, chopped

2 16-oz. cans kidney beans, drained and rinsed

2 16-oz. cans pinto beans, drained and rinsed

2 15-oz. cans diced tomatoes

15-oz. can diced tomatoes with green chiles

2 6-oz. cans tomato paste

2 T. chili powder

2 T. salt

Optional: 3 to 4 c. water

Garnish: shredded Cheddar cheese

GRILLED VEGGIE SAMMIES

AMY THOMASON HUNT
TRAPHILL, NC

Oh-so good and cheesy! Delicious just the way it is, or add some thin-sliced cooked chicken for a hearty sandwich.

1 small zucchini, cut
   into 4 thin slices
   lengthwise
2 portabella mushroom
   caps, cut in half
2 T. olive oil
salt and pepper to taste
1 loaf French bread,
   halved lengthwise
1 large tomato, cut into
   4 slices
4 slices smoked
   provolone cheese
8 fresh basil or spinach
   leaves

Brush zucchini and mushrooms with olive oil; sprinkle with salt and pepper. Place on a preheated grill and close lid. Grill for 5 to 7 minutes, turning once, until tender. Spread cut sides of bread with Lemon-Garlic Mayonnaise. On bottom half of loaf, layer zucchini, mushrooms, tomato, cheese and basil or spinach leaves. Add top of loaf; cut into 4 pieces.

Lemon-Garlic Mayonnaise:

In a small bowl, mix all ingredients until well combined.

Makes 4 sandwiches.

**LEMON-GARLIC
MAYONNAISE**
1/4 c. mayonnaise
1 t. garlic, minced
1 T. lemon juice

ITALIAN BEEF IN A BUCKET

CAROL BOBENG
RALEIGH, NC

This is a family favorite and is a "must" at every gathering. My son makes it, my daughter makes it and last time, my oldest grandson prepared it. Hope it becomes a favorite in your family, too!

Place beef roast in a large slow cooker. In a bowl, combine remaining ingredients except rolls; do not drain pepperoncini. Pour mixture over roast. Cover and cook on low setting for 10 to 12 hours, until meat is very tender. Shred with 2 forks; stir into mixture in slow cooker. Serve on rolls; top with some of the giardiniera mixture from the slow cooker.

Makes 12 to 18 servings.

3-1/2 to 4-lb. beef rump roast
12-oz. jar Italian giardiniera mix, mild or hot, drained
12-oz. jar pepperoncini
.7-oz. pkg. zesty Italian salad dressing mix
10-1/2 oz. can beef broth
12 to 18 crusty Italian rolls, split

GRILLED PEPPER JACK SANDWICHES

AMY THOMASON HUNT
TRAPHILL, NC

I adapted this from another recipe to suit our tastes...we like it!

Thoroughly blend butter and taco seasoning. Spread butter mixture on one side of each slice of bread. Heat a large skillet or griddle over medium heat. Place 4 bread slices in skillet, butter-side down; top each with a cheese slice. Top with remaining bread slices, butter-side up. Cook until bread is golden and cheese is melted, turning once.

Makes 4 sandwiches.

4 T. butter, softened
8 slices bread
2 t. taco seasoning mix
4 slices Pepper Jack cheese

DOWN-HOME SPLIT PEA SOUP

JUDE TRIMNAL
BREVARD, NC

This classic soup is easy to make in the electric pressure cooker. The split peas cook quickly and the vegetables keep their color.

1 T. olive oil

1 c. celery, sliced

1-1/2 c. carrot, peeled and sliced

1/2 c. onion, chopped

2 c. dried split peas

8 c. chicken or vegetable broth

1-1/2 c. cooked ham, cubed

1/4 t. nutmeg

salt and pepper to taste

lemon juice to taste

Choose the Sauté setting and heat the oil. Add the celery, carrot and onion and cook until vegetables are softened, about 5 minutes. Stir in peas, broth, ham and nutmeg. Press Cancel to reset pot. Secure the lid and set pressure release to Sealing. Choose Manual/Pressure and set on high pressure for 20 minutes. After cooking time is up, allow the pressure to release naturally for 20 minutes, then release remaining pressure manually using the Venting/Quick Release method. Carefully open the lid. Add salt and pepper to taste. Stir in a little lemon juice right before serving.

Serves 8

KITCHEN TIP

For thick, creamy vegetable soup, use a hand-held immersion blender to purée some of the cooked veggies right in the stockpot.

CLAM CHOWDER

JEWEL SHARPE
RALEIGH, NC

A tried & true recipe I like to use in cool weather when we go camping. So simple...so delicious!

Combine all ingredients except crackers in a slow cooker. Cover and cook on low setting for 2 to 4 hours. Serve with crackers.

Makes 6 to 8 servings.

3 10-3/4 oz. cans cream of potato soup

2 10-3/4 oz. cans New England clam chowder

1 pt. half-and-half

2 6-1/2 oz. cans chopped clams

1/2 c. onion, diced

1/2 c. butter, sliced

Garnish: saltine crackers

SOUTHERN BBQ

CYNDI LITTLE
WHITSETT, NC

Serve this either as a main dish with sides or on hamburger buns with slaw for a truly great North Carolina-style meal.

Mix together vinegar, sugar and salt. Pour over roast in a slow cooker. Cover and cook on low setting for 10 to 12 hours, until meat pulls from bones. Remove roast and cool; pull apart and shred. Mix 6 to 8 tablespoons of cooking liquid with Worcestershire sauce and catsup. Pour over pork and add hot sauce to taste, if desired; mix well. Spoon shredded pork and sauce onto buns.

Makes 6 to 8 sandwiches.

1 c. cider vinegar

2 T. sugar

1 T. salt

3 to 4-lb. pork loin roast

1 T. Worcestershire sauce

1/2 c. catsup

Optional: hot sauce to taste

6 to 8 sandwich buns, split

CHAPTER FOUR

CAROLINA MOUNTAIN
Mains

FILL THEM UP WITH A STICK-TO-THE-RIBS MEAL THAT IS FULL OF FLAVOR AND HEARTY ENOUGH TO SATISFY EVEN THE BIGGEST APPETITE.

SLOPPY JOE CASSEROLE

**AMY THOMASON HUNT
TRAPHILL, NC**

This is a less messy way to eat a Sloppy Joe, but just as good. Creamy comfort food. This smells wonderful while it's cooking!

1 lb. ground beef
1 onion, diced
1 green pepper, diced
salt to taste
10-3/4 oz. can tomato soup
1/2 c. water
1 t. Worcestershire sauce
7-1/2 oz. tube refrigerated biscuits
1/2 c. shredded Cheddar cheese

Brown beef with onion, pepper and salt in a skillet over medium heat; drain. Stir in soup, water and Worcestershire sauce; heat to a boil. Spoon beef mixture into a greased 1-1/2 quart casserole dish. Arrange biscuits on top of beef mixture around the edges of the dish. Bake, uncovered, at 400 degrees for 15 minutes, or until biscuits are golden. Sprinkle cheese over biscuits; bake again for 15 minutes, or until cheese is melted.

Serves 4.

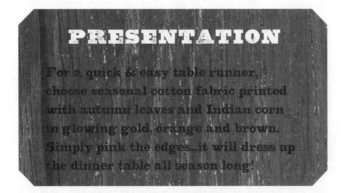

PRESENTATION

For a quick & easy table runner, choose seasonal cotton fabric printed with autumn leaves and Indian corn in glowing gold, orange and brown. Simply pink the edges...it will dress up the dinner table all season long!

THELMA'S PORK CHOPS

**SHIRL PARSONS
CAPE CARTERET, NC**

*This is a recipe from my husband's grandmother, Thelma Skelton.
She was well-known as a great cook. One taste and you'll see why!*

Season pork chops with salt and pepper; roll in cornmeal or flour. Heat oil in a large skillet over medium heat. Add chops, working in batches if necessary; brown chops on both sides. Arrange chops in a lightly greased 3-quart casserole dish; set aside. In a bowl, whisk together soup and water; spoon over chops. Sprinkle with soup mix, if desired. Cover and bake at 325 degrees for 45 to 50 minutes, until chops are tender.

Makes 6 to 8 servings.

6 to 8 pork chops
salt and pepper to taste
1 c. cornmeal or all-purpose flour
4 to 5 T. olive oil
10-3/4 oz. can cream of mushroom soup
1/2 c. water
Optional: 1.35-oz. pkg. onion soup mix

BAKED QUESADILLAS

PATTI WALKER
MOCKSVILLE, NC

Quesadillas are a nice change from tacos. Sometimes we make these only with cheese. My children enjoy them as a meal or as a quick snack.

2 8-oz. cans chicken, drained and flaked

1 to 2 T. taco seasoning mix

8-oz. jar salsa

8-oz. pkg. shredded Mexican-blend cheese

16 8-inch flour tortillas

Garnish: sour cream, avocado slices

Mix chicken, taco seasoning, salsa and cheese. Arrange 8 tortillas on baking sheets sprayed with non-stick vegetable spray. Spread chicken mixture onto tortillas. Top with remaining tortillas. Spray tops with non-stick vegetable spray. Bake at 350 degrees for 5 to 10 minutes, until tops are golden. Allow to cool for a few minutes; cut into quarters. Garnish with sour cream and avocado slices.

Makes 8 servings.

Buttermilk Fried Chicken, p87

Whether you are looking for a quick breakfast to start the day off right, no-fuss party fare for those special guests, satisfying soups and sandwiches for the perfect lunch, main dishes to bring them to the table fast, or a sweet little something to savor at the end of the meal, you'll love these recipes from the amazing cooks in beautiful North Carolina.

Cheese Pound Cake, p128

Nacho Chicken Dip, p114

an Asparagus, p33

Banana-Mango Soy Smoothie, p20

Baked Quesadillas, p80

Make-Ahead Pumpkin Pie French Toast, p2

Bran & Raisin Muffins, p8

Peanutty Breakfast Wrap, p16

Pulled Pork Barbecue, p54

Blueberry Buckwheat Pancakes, p22

...ch on a Stick, p115

...t Twists, p24

Roquefort Cut-Out Crackers, p114

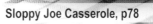

Sloppy Joe Casserole, p78

Game-Day Sandwich, p55

Roland's Barbecued Spareribs, p100

Down-Home Split Pea Soup, p74

Brown Sugar Puddin' Pies, p128

st North Carolina Pulled Pork BBQ, p58

Garlicky Savory Parmesan Asparagus, p36

Paprika Beef & Noodles, p88

Winter Barbecued Chicken, p89

Pineapple Casserole, p32

Coconut-Orange Breakfast Rolls, p9

BUTTERMILK FRIED CHICKEN

CYNDI LITTLE
WHITSETT, NC

My daddy made amazing fried chicken, but he passed away when I was 12. It's taken me a long time to make chicken that I feel is almost as good as his.

Combine chicken and buttermilk in a large bowl. Cover and refrigerate for one hour. Meanwhile, combine flour, salt and pepper in a large plastic zipping bag. Drain chicken, discarding buttermilk. Working in batches, add chicken to bag and toss to coat. Shake off excess flour and let chicken rest for 15 minutes. Heat 1/4 inch of oil in a large skillet over medium heat. Fry chicken in oil until golden on all sides. Reduce heat to medium-low; cover and simmer, turning occasionally, for 40 to 45 minutes, until juices run clear. Uncover and cook 5 minutes longer.

Serves 4 to 6.

2-1/2 lbs. chicken
1 c. buttermilk
1 c. all-purpose flour
1-1/2 t. salt
1/2 t. pepper
oil for frying

PAPRIKA BEEF & NOODLES

TERESA PEARMAN
MARSHALL, NC

*My mom always made this delicious meal during the cold winter
months...it always warms you up.*

1-3/4 c. water, divided
2 lbs. stew beef cubes
1 c. onion, sliced
1 clove garlic, diced
3/4 c. catsup
2 T. Worcestershire
  sauce
1 T. brown sugar,
  packed
2 t. salt
2 t. paprika
1/8 t. dry mustard
1/8 t. cayenne pepper
2 T. all-purpose flour
cooked egg noodles

In a slow cooker, combine 1-1/2 cups water and remaining ingredients except flour and noodles; mix well. Cover and cook on low setting for 6 to 8 hours. In a cup, stir together remaining water and flour. Drizzle into beef mixture; stir. Cook, uncovered, until thickened. Serve beef mixture over noodles.

Serves 6 to 8.

WINTER BARBECUED CHICKEN

MIA ROSSI
CHARLOTTE, NC

Can't wait for barbecued chicken? You don't have to with this simple slow-cooker recipe. Now you can enjoy mouthwatering barbecued chicken any time of year!

In a bowl, stir together seasonings. Place chicken pieces in a slow cooker and sprinkle with seasoning mixture; toss to coat. In a separate bowl, whisk together remaining ingredients except lemon. Pour cola mixture over chicken; place lemon slices on top. Cover and cook on low setting for 6 to 7 hours, until chicken juices run clear. Remove chicken to a serving platter and discard lemon. Spoon sauce in slow cooker over chicken.

Serves 6 to 8.

1-1/2 t. paprika
1/2 t. garlic powder
2 t. salt
1/2 t. pepper
3 lbs. chicken
1/2 c. cola
1/3 c. catsup
1/4 c. light brown sugar, packed
2 T. cider vinegar
Optional: 2 T. bourbon
1 lemon, sliced

GARDEN-TO-TABLE SPINACH-ALFREDO PIZZA

AMY THOMASON HUNT
TRAPHILL, NC

*This is a must on my farmhouse table whenever my best friend
Sue comes for a visit. I think you'll love it too!*

6-1/2 oz. pkg. pizza crust mix

1/2 to 3/4 c. basil and garlic **Alfredo** sauce

4 c. fresh spinach, chopped

2 tomatoes, diced

1/2 c. sliced mushrooms

1/2 c. red onion, diced

8-oz. pkg. shredded pizza-blend cheese

Prepare crust mix according to package directions. Spread dough on a 12" round pizza pan coated with non-stick vegetable spray. Spread Alfredo sauce over dough, leaving a one-inch edge. Top with spinach, tomatoes, mushrooms and onion; sprinkle with cheese. Bake at 450 degrees for 10 to 15 minutes, until cheese is melted and crust is golden. Let stand for several minutes; cut into wedges or squares.

Makes 4 to 6 servings.

KITCHEN TIP

For thick and creamy casseroles, try using dry bread crumbs instead of adding flour.

MOM'S SALMON PATTIES

DARCY ANDERS
HENDERSONVILLE, NC

For as long as I can remember, my grandmother and mother made these salmon patties for our family. They were always a favorite of mine as a child. They are now my daughter's favorite too...like mother, like daughter!

Place salmon in a bowl; flake with a fork. Add egg, flour, onion, lemon juice, Worcestershire sauce, parsley, crushed potato chips and enough of reserved salmon liquid to moisten. Mix with fork until blended. Add more crushed chips if mixture becomes too moist. Form into 4 flattened patties. Heat oil in a skillet over medium heat. Add patties and cook until golden on both sides. Serve with lemon wedges.

Makes 4 servings.

15-oz. can red salmon, drained and liquid reserved

1 egg, lightly beaten

2 T. all-purpose flour

2 T. onion, finely chopped

2 T. lemon juice

1 t. Worcestershire sauce

1/4 t. fresh parsley, chopped

1/2 c. potato chips, crushed

1 to 2 T. oil

Garnish: lemon wedges

BBQ CHICKEN FLATBREAD

JENNIFER RUBINO
HICKORY, NC

The flavor of barbecue chicken reminds me of campfires and smoke pits. Serve sliced apples with a caramel dipping sauce for dessert, and you've got all the flavors of fall. Happy fall, y'all!

4 flatbreads
6 T. barbecue sauce
24 slices deli oven-roasted chicken
1 c. shredded Cheddar cheese

Place each flatbread on a piece of foil; arrange on baking sheets. Spread each flatbread with 1-1/2 tablespoons barbecue sauce; layer with 6 slices of chicken. Sprinkle cheese over all. Bake at 350 degrees for 5 minutes, or until cheese is melted.

Makes 4 servings.

CREAMY PESTO & BOWTIES

CHERYLANN SMITH
ELFLAND, NC

My kids love this! It's great on a cold day.

1 lb. boneless, skinless chicken breasts
2 T. butter
8-oz. pkg. bowtie pasta, uncooked and divided
10-3/4 oz. can cream of celery soup
1/2 c. pesto sauce
1/2 c. milk

In a skillet over medium heat, cook chicken in butter until golden and juices run clear. Meanwhile, cook pasta according to package directions; drain. Set aside and cover to keep warm. Stir remaining ingredients into chicken; bring to a boil. Reduce heat and simmer 5 minutes. Stir in pasta and heat through.

Serves 4.

LEMON-RICE STUFFED COD & BROCCOLINI

MIA ROSSI
CHARLOTTE, NC

By tradition, my Italian family always has seafood on Christmas Eve. It's often an elaborate dinner, but with this easy recipe I can serve up an all-in-one meal that everyone enjoys. Great for other busy days too.

In a large saucepan over medium heat, sauté onion and celery in butter. Add water, salt and thyme; stir in uncooked rice. Reduce heat to medium-low. Cover and simmer until rice is tender, 15 to 25 minutes. Remove from heat; stir in yogurt. Dice half of lemon and add to rice mixture; set aside. Drizzle broccolini with olive oil; add seasonings and set aside. With a thin knife, slice each fish fillet on one long edge without cutting all the way through; open up flat. Divide rice mixture evenly among fillets, placing to one side; fold other half over to close. Place stuffed fillets on a greased baking sheet. Bake, uncovered, at 350 degrees for 25 to 30 minutes, adding broccolini to pan after 10 minutes. Thinly slice remaining lemon; garnish cod and broccolini with lemon.

Serves 6.

1/4 c. onion, chopped
1/4 c. celery, diced
2 T. butter
1 c. hot water
1/8 t. salt
1/8 t. dried thyme
3/4 c. long-cooking rice, uncooked
1 c. plain yogurt
1 lemon, peeled and halved
1 lb. broccolini, trimmed
2 T. olive oil
garlic salt and pepper to taste
6 6-oz. codfish fillets

STUFFED POBLANO PEPPERS

RENEE HOPFER
STOKESDALE, NC

My husband loves chiles relleno and orders them every time we go out for Mexican food. I wanted to make a similar type of dish at home and came up with this recipe.

6.8-oz. pkg. Spanish rice- flavored rice vermicelli mix

10-oz. can diced tomatoes with green chiles

1 lb. lean ground beef

salt and pepper to taste

8-oz. pkg. shredded Mexican-blend cheese, divided

6 large poblano peppers

Garnish: tortilla chips, sour cream, salsa

Prepare Spanish rice mix according package directions. Before turning rice mix down to simmer, stir in tomatoes with chiles. Meanwhile, in a large skillet over medium heat, brown beef and drain. Season beef with salt and pepper. When rice is done, add rice to beef along with 1/2 cup shredded cheese. Mix well. Slice down one side of each pepper; remove stem caps and seeds. Fill peppers generously with rice mixture. Arrange peppers in a greased 2-quart casserole dish. Cover with aluminum foil. Bake at 350 degrees for 35 to 45 minutes, checking after 25 minutes, until peppers are tender. Uncover; top peppers with cheese and re-cover with foil. Bake an additional 5 to 7 minutes, until cheese is melted. Serve with tortilla chips, sour cream and salsa.

Makes 6 servings.

SUNDAY BUTTERMILK ROAST

AMY THOMASON HUNT
TRAPHILL, NC

This is a tender and juicy roast that's great for Sunday suppers and church dinners. It includes veggies and makes its own gravy...all you need to add is dessert!

Place roast in a lightly greased Dutch oven; sprinkle with soup mix, salt and pepper. Arrange vegetables around roast; pour buttermilk over roast. Cover and bake at 350 degrees for 2-1/2 to 3 hours, until roast is done. Transfer roast and vegetables to a serving platter; cover to keep warm. Skim fat from pan drippings. Pour drippings into a saucepan; bring to a boil over medium heat. Cook, stirring occasionally, until liquid is reduced to about one cup. Serve gravy with sliced roast and vegetables.

Serves 8.

- 3-lb. boneless beef London broil or other roast
- 1-oz. pkg. onion soup mix
- salt and pepper to taste
- 8 to 10 redskin potatoes, halved
- 8 carrots, peeled and cut in half lengthwise
- 6 small white onions, quartered
- 1 c. buttermilk

HONEY-MUSTARD SALMON

CAROL CREEL
RALEIGH, NC

Super-simple and oh-so tasty! I serve this with sweet potato fries.

In a small bowl, mix mustard, honey and lemon juice. Spread mixture over each piece of fish; sprinkle with pepper. Place fish in 2 to 4 aluminum foil pouches; crimp to seal pouches. Grill, covered, over medium-high heat for 10 to 12 minutes, until fish flakes easily with a fork. May also bake packets on baking sheets at 400 degrees for 15 to 20 minutes.

Makes 4 servings.

- 2 t. Dijon mustard
- 1 T. honey
- 3 T. lemon juice
- 1 lb. skinless salmon fillet, cut into 4 pieces
- pepper to taste

SHRIMP SCAMPI & ASPARAGUS

LINDA KARNER
PISGAH FOREST, NC

We love fresh asparagus when it comes in season, and I always try to find new ways of using it. This is a recipe I came up with...my husband just loves it!

16-oz. pkg. linguine
  pasta, uncooked
1 T. salt
2 T. butter
2 T. olive oil
1 lb. asparagus,
  trimmed and cut into
  bite-size pieces
2 cloves garlic, minced
2 lbs. medium shrimp,
  peeled and cleaned
2 T. mixed fresh herbs
  like basil, thyme,
  oregano and chives,
  chopped
2 T. capers, drained
juice of 1/2 lemon
salt and pepper to taste
Optional: 1 T. additional
  butter and/or olive oil
1/2 c. shredded
  Parmesan cheese,
  divided

Cook pasta according to package directions, adding salt to cooking water; drain when pasta is just tender. Meanwhile, in a large skillet over medium heat, melt butter with olive oil. Add asparagus and sauté until partially tender, about 5 minutes. Stir in garlic and shrimp. Cook until shrimp is bright pink, about 5 to 7 minutes. Add herbs, capers and lemon juice; heat through. Season with salt and pepper. Add pasta to mixture in skillet; toss well. If desired, stir in additional butter and/or olive oil. Add 1/4 cup Parmesan cheese and toss again. Serve garnished with remaining cheese.

Makes 6 servings.

SHRIMP SOFT TACOS

SHIRL PARSONS
CAPE CARTERET, NC

A light tropical-inspired meal that can be prepared in no time... delicious!

Spray a skillet with non-stick vegetable spray. Over medium-high heat, sauté pepper, onion and garlic for 2 minutes. Add shrimp, tomatoes and seasonings; sauté for 3 minutes, or until shrimp are no longer pink. Stir in cilantro. Top each tortilla with 1/4 cup shrimp mixture, 3 tablespoons cheese and 2 tablespoons Tropical Salsa; fold over.

Tropical Salsa:

Mix all ingredients in a bowl; cover and chill.

Makes 8 servings.

1 c. yellow peppers, sliced
1 c. red onion, sliced
1 clove garlic, minced
1-1/2 lbs. medium shrimp, cleaned
1 c. tomatoes, chopped
1/2 t. ground cumin
1/2 t. chili powder
2 T. fresh cilantro, chopped
8 6-inch flour tortillas
1-1/4 c. shredded low-fat Monterey Jack cheese

TROPICAL SALSA

11-oz. can mandarin oranges, drained
8-oz. can pineapple tidbits, drained
1/4 c. green onions, chopped
1 T. chopped green chiles
1 T. fresh cilantro, chopped
1 T. lemon juice

TANGY BBQ CHICKEN

JEWEL SHARPE
RALEIGH, NC

The barbecue sauce in this recipe is our family favorite...I could almost drink it! The recipe makes about 1-1/2 cups sauce that's tasty on chicken, beef and pork.

1 c. brewed coffee
1 c. catsup
1/2 c. sugar
1/2 c. Worcestershire sauce
1/4 c. cider vinegar
1/8 t. pepper
8 chicken legs with thighs

In a saucepan, combine all ingredients except chicken. Bring to a boil over medium heat; reduce heat to low. Simmer, uncovered, for 30 to 35 minutes until thickened, stirring occasionally. Grill chicken as desired, brushing with sauce as it cooks.

Makes 8 servings.

LEMON HERB & GARLIC SHRIMP

CHERYLANN SMITH
ELFLAND, NC

This shrimp dish is often requested by my children....and when Daddy isn't looking, they sneak shrimp off his plate!

2 cloves garlic, pressed
2 T. olive oil
6 T. butter, sliced
1 lb. frozen cooked shrimp
1.8-oz. pkg. lemon herb soup mix
1 c. warm water

In a skillet over medium heat, sauté garlic in olive oil and butter for 2 minutes. Add shrimp and simmer until shrimp thaws, stirring often. Dissolve soup mix in water; pour over shrimp mixture. Reduce heat; simmer until heated through, about 20 minutes.

Makes 4 to 6 servings.

BALSAMIC CHICKEN & PENNE

MARY NEHRING
BELMONT, NC

I like fresh asparagus in this recipe, but my kids don't care for it, so sometimes I substitute fresh green beans...they'll eat those!

In a large plastic zipping bag, combine olive oil, balsamic vinegar, mustard, sugar, garlic and seasonings. Squeeze bag to mix well. Add chicken to bag; turn to coat. Seal bag and refrigerate at least 4 hours to overnight, turning bag occasionally. When ready to prepare chicken, drain marinade into a saucepan; heat to boiling for 15 minutes. Meanwhile, cook pasta according to package directions; drain. Broil chicken until chicken juices run clear, about 12 to 15 minutes. Cut chicken into bite-size pieces. To serve, combine chicken, marinade, asparagus and pasta. Toss to coat. Serve with Parmesan cheese,if desired.

Makes 8 servings.

1/2 c. extra-virgin olive oil

1/4 c. balsamic vinegar

2 T. country Dijon mustard

2 T. sugar

3 cloves garlic, minced

1/2 t. salt

1/4 t. cayenne pepper, or to taste

4 boneless, skinless chicken breasts

8-oz. pkg. whole-wheat penne pasta, uncooked

1 bunch asparagus, trimmed, chopped and steamed

Optional: shredded Parmesan cheese

ROLAND'S BARBECUED SPARERIBS

JANET DUMAS
RALEIGH, NC

This is our Christmas tradition. My father, Roland Lambert, used to make these spareribs for Christmas every year and boy, did they taste good! He liked to cook after he retired. My mom would help make the sauce with him. You couldn't rush the ribs...they are wonderful.

3 to 4 lbs. pork baby back ribs, cut into serving-size sections

1 lemon, peeled and thinly sliced

1 onion, thinly sliced

2 c. water

1 c. catsup

1/3 c. Worcestershire sauce

1 t. chili powder

1 t. salt

3/8 t. hot pepper sauce

Place ribs meaty-side up in a shallow roasting pan; top with lemon and onion slices. Bake, uncovered, at 450 degrees for 30 minutes; pour off any drippings. Meanwhile, combine remaining ingredients in a saucepan over medium heat. Bring to a boil, stirring often. Spoon sauce over ribs. Bake, uncovered, at 350 degrees for one hour, or until tender, turning and basting often with sauce.

Makes 4 to 6 servings.

BALSAMIC CHICKEN

**GINGER JONES
ROSMAN, NC**

This is a light recipe with lots of flavor. It's very simple to make.

Pour olive oil into a 3-quart slow cooker, spreading to coat the bottom. Add remaining ingredients except pasta in the order listed; do not drain tomatoes. Cover and cook on low setting for 3 to 5 hours, or on high setting for 2 to 3 hours. Check chicken occasionally for doneness. Serve chicken over cooked pasta.

Makes 4 to 6 servings.

2 T. extra-virgin olive oil

4 to 6 boneless, skinless chicken breasts

1 onion, thinly sliced

8-oz. jar sliced mushrooms, drained

4-oz. can sliced black olives, drained

1 t. dried basil

1 t. dried oregano

1 t. dried rosemary

1/2 t. dried thyme

salt and pepper to taste

1/2 c. balsamic vinegar

14-1/2 oz. can crushed tomatoes

cooked angel hair pasta

MANDARIN ORANGE CHICKEN

BETH BRUNER
BROADWAY, NC

A friend gave me this recipe, and it's now one of my favorites. It's such a delicious and easy change from the same humdrum slow-cooker chicken dishes.

- 2 lbs. boneless, skinless chicken breasts
- 2 carrots, peeled and sliced 1/2-inch thick
- 2 red and/or green peppers, cut into 1/2-inch chunks
- 3 cloves garlic, minced
- 2 t. ground ginger
- 1 t. salt
- 1/2 t. pepper
- 8-oz. can frozen orange juice concentrate
- 2 c. cooked rice
- 2 11-oz. cans mandarin oranges, drained
- 2 green onions, chopped

Combine chicken, carrots, peppers, garlic, seasonings and orange juice concentrate in a slow cooker; mix well. Cover and cook on low setting for 4 to 6 hours, until chicken is no longer pink in the center. Arrange chicken over rice on a serving plate; top with oranges and green onions. Drizzle with some sauce from slow cooker, if desired.

Serves 4.

EASY-PEASY BOLOGNESE SAUCE

VICKIE
GOOSEBERRY PATCH

This authentic Italian sauce is a snap to cook up in the slow cooker. It has a deep, rich flavor that really shines through with the longer cook time...perfect over your favorite pasta.

Cook bacon in a large skillet over medium heat until just crisp. Add oil, onion, celery and carrots; cook until vegetables are tender, about 5 minutes. Add beef; sprinkle with salt and pepper. Continue cooking until beef is almost completely browned, about 10 minutes; drain. Add wine or broth; cook for 3 to 4 minutes. Transfer beef mixture to a slow cooker; add tomatoes with juice and bay leaves. Cover and cook on low setting for 6 hours; season again with salt and pepper. Discard bay leaves; stir in half-and-half and parsley just before serving.

Makes 10 to 12 servings.

1/4 lb. bacon, chopped
1 T. olive oil
1 onion, minced
3/4 c. celery, minced
2 carrots, peeled and minced
2 lbs. lean ground beef
salt and pepper to taste
1/4 c. white wine or chicken broth
2 28-oz. cans crushed tomatoes
3 bay leaves
1/2 c. half-and-half
1/4 c. fresh parsley, chopped

ROSEMARY-GARLIC SKILLET PORK & POTATOES

MICHELLE BURKE
THOMASVILLE, NC

The day we moved into our new house, it was snowing really hard. We had only my cast-iron skillet unpacked, and just a few ingredients in our pantry. I was able to make a yummy meal for my three boys and hubby to enjoy... and hardly any clean-up!

2 T. plus 2 t. olive oil, divided
1-lb. pork tenderloin
2 to 3 lbs. new redskin potatoes, halved
1/2 to 1 lb. baby carrots
3 cloves garlic, chopped
2 t. fresh rosemary, snipped
salt and pepper to taste

Heat 2 teaspoons oil in a cast-iron skillet over medium heat. Brown pork on all sides. Arrange potatoes and carrots around pork; drizzle with remaining oil. Sprinkle garlic and rosemary over all; season with salt and pepper. Transfer skillet to oven. Bake, uncovered, at 375 minutes for 45 minutes. Remove from oven; let stand for 5 minutes before serving.

Serves 4 to 5.

AUNT RUTH'S MUSHROOM CHICKEN

REBECCA WILSON
BESSEMER CITY, NC

My Maw-Maw's sister lived about 1-1/2 hours away, which to a kid is quite a distance! We would drive up on a Sunday and this slow-cooker chicken was one of the many things she would fix for us.

6 boneless, skinless chicken breasts
10-3/4 oz. can cream of mushroom soup
16-oz. container sour cream
1.35-oz. pkg. onion soup mix
cooked rice

Place chicken in a slow cooker. In a bowl, mix together remaining ingredients except rice; spoon over chicken. Cover and cook on high setting for 4 to 6 hours, until chicken is cooked through. Serve with cooked rice.

Serves 6.

SPICY SHREDDED BEEF TOSTADAS

NIKKI JUDD
CHARLOTTE, NC

I have four kids who all like to eat different things. This is one of the few recipes they unanimously agree on! If you don't like spicy food, just use one can of peppers in adobo sauce.

Bring roast to room temperature; sprinkle with salt and pepper. Heat oil in a skillet over medium heat; add roast to skillet and brown on all sides. Place roast in a slow cooker. In a bowl, mix peppers with sauce, tomato sauce and seasonings. Pour mixture over beef. Cover and cook on low setting for 8 to 10 hours, or on high setting for about 6 hours. Shred roast with 2 forks; mix well with sauce in slow cooker. Serve on tostadas or taco shells, topped as desired.

Serves 8 to 10.

3 to 4-lb. beef chuck roast
salt and pepper to taste
1 to 2 T. canola oil
1 to 2 7-oz. cans chipotle peppers in adobo sauce
15-oz. can tomato sauce
1 t. ground cumin
1 t. coriander
1 t. garlic powder
2 t. dried, minced onion
tostadas or taco shells
Toppings: sour cream, shredded cheese, chopped tomatoes, shredded lettuce

PAN-FRIED CHICKEN THIGHS

**JO ANN
GOOSEBERRY PATCH**

*My family loves this tender, golden chicken. I've come to prefer chicken
thighs over boneless chicken breasts, as they're so much more flavorful...
cheaper too! Serve with mashed potatoes.*

**1 yellow onion, chopped
4 cloves garlic, minced
8 sprigs fresh thyme
1/2 t. salt
1/2 t. pepper
3 T. olive oil, divided
6 to 8 chicken thighs**

In a large bowl, combine onion, garlic, thyme, salt
and pepper. Stir in one tablespoon oil; add chicken
and turn to coat well. Heat remaining oil in a large
heavy skillet over medium heat for 2 minutes. Add
chicken to skillet, skin-side down. Spoon onion
mixture in bowl over chicken. Cook for 10 minutes,
stirring occasionally. Turn chicken over; stir mixture
in skillet. Cook another 5 to 6 minutes, until chicken
juices run clear when pierced.

Makes 6 to 8 servings.

CITRUS PARTY FISH

**MIA ROSSI
CHARLOTTE, NC**

*My family's version of the traditional Italian fish dinner! We like to serve
this quick & easy (and might I add tasty!) dish on Christmas Eve, just
before opening presents.*

**1-1/2 lbs. tilapia fillets
salt and pepper to taste
5 T. fresh parsley,
  chopped
1 onion, chopped
4 t. oil
2 t. lemon zest
2 t. orange zest
Garnish: orange and
  lemon slices**

Season fish fillets with salt and pepper; place in a
lightly greased slow cooker. Place parsley, onion, oil
and zest over fish. Cover and cook on low setting for
1-1/2 hours. Garnish with orange and lemon slices.

Serves 6 to 8.

POTLUCK PIZZA CASSEROLE

**SHEILA PLOCK
LELAND, NC**

I took this casserole to many Cub Scout banquets! A great take-along dish for a family potluck dinner.

Cook pastas together according to package directions, just until tender; drain. Meanwhile, brown beef with onion and green pepper in a large skillet over medium heat; drain. Add pepperoni and mushrooms. Simmer over medium-low heat for 15 minutes, stirring occasionally. Add cooked macaroni and spaghetti sauce to skillet; heat through. Transfer to a lightly greased 3-quart casserole dish; sprinkle with cheese. Bake at 350 degrees for 15 minutes, or until bubbly and cheese melts.

Makes 6 servings.

1 c. shell pasta, uncooked
1 c. rotini pasta, uncooked
1 c. elbow macaroni, uncooked
1 lb. ground beef
3/4 c. onion, diced
3/4 c. green pepper, diced
1/2 lb. sliced turkey pepperoni
8-oz. jar sliced mushrooms, drained
24-oz. jar spaghetti sauce
8-oz. pkg. shredded mozzarella cheese

DINNERTIME CONVERSATION

"Sugar" Ray Leonard, considered one of the greatest boxers of all time and an Olympic gold medalist in 1976, was born in Wilmington, North Carolina.

CORN CHIP CHICKEN

LYNN LONG
GREENSBORO, NC

I found this recipe over 20 years ago on the back of a shredded cheese package. It has been served for many children's birthdays and weekly meals. It is always the dinner requested when the kids have a friend over for dinner. I always double the recipe...the next morning, everyone wants the leftovers for breakfast!

4 boneless, skinless
  chicken breasts,
  flattened to 1/2-inch
  thick
10-3/4 oz. can cream of
  chicken soup
3/4 c. milk
1-oz. pkg. taco seasoning
  mix
8-oz. pkg. shredded
  sharp Cheddar cheese
6-oz. pkg. corn chips
cooked brown rice

Arrange chicken in a 13"x9" baking pan coated with non-stick vegetable spray. In a bowl, combine soup, milk, taco seasoning and cheese; spoon over chicken. Top chicken with corn chips; cover with aluminum foil. Bake at 350 degrees for 50 minutes, or until chicken juices run clear when pierced. Serve with cooked rice.

Makes 4 servings.

BEEF SUPPER IN A SKILLET

RITA FRYE
KING, NC

This isn't a Christmas recipe as such, but I do fix it often during the hectic holidays when time for a sit-down dinner is a luxury. It comes together in less than 30 minutes, is warm and hearty, and a family favorite! I set the skillet on a trivet right on the table, and serve with a dark green leafy salad and cinnamon applesauce. My family always squirts catsup on their portions.

Cook macaroni according to package directions; drain well. Meanwhile; brown beef in a large skillet; drain. Place bacon on a microwave-safe dish between several paper towels; microwave on high for 4 to 5 minutes. Stir soup and crumbled or chopped bacon into beef; add cooked macaroni and stir well. Spread cheese on top. Cover skillet and let stand until cheese melts, or put skillet under the broiler for a few minutes. Serve with catsup on the side, if desired.

Serves 6.

8-oz. pkg. elbow
 macaroni, uncooked
1 lb. ground beef
4 to 5 slices bacon
10-1/2 oz. can tomato
 soup
8-oz. pkg. shredded
 sharp Cheddar cheese
Optional: catsup

DINNERTIME CONVERSATION

The luxurious Biltmore Estate in Asheville is the largest private chateau in the world. Built in 1895 by George Biltmore, it features 250 rooms, extensive gardens and an award-winning winery. More than 1.7 million visitors tour Biltmore every year.

CHICKEN CORDON BLEU

**LINDA HARMON,
GARNER, NC**

*If you love traditional Chicken Cordon Bleu, give this easy slow-cooker
version a try! Chicken, ham and Swiss cheese slow-simmered for hours in
a creamy sauce...mmm.*

**10-3/4 oz. can cream of
chicken soup**

1 c. milk

**4 to 6 boneless, skinless
chicken breasts**

1/4 lb. sliced deli ham

**1/4 lb. sliced Swiss
cheese**

In a bowl, combine soup and milk. Pour enough of
soup mixture into a slow cooker to cover the bottom;
arrange chicken over top. Cover chicken with slices
of ham and cheese. Pour remaining soup mixture
over cheese. Cover and cook on low setting for 4
to 6 hours, or on high setting for 2 to 3 hours, until
chicken juices run clear when pierced.

Serves 4 to 6

CHICKEN-ALMOND CASSEROLE

**SHIRL PARSONS
CAPE CARTERET, NC**

This was a favorite recipe of Granny Skelton's, my husband's grandmother. It's delicious...good enough for company.

In a large bowl, stir together chicken, soup, sour cream, mayonnaise and seasonings. Add water chestnuts, mushrooms, celery and onion; mix until well blended. Transfer to a greased 13"x9" baking pan; sprinkle with cheese. In a small bowl, toss crackers with melted butter; sprinkle over cheese and top with almonds. Bake, uncovered, at 350 degrees for 25 to 30 minutes, until hot and bubbly.

Makes 8 servings.

- 3 c. cooked chicken, cubed
- 10-3/4 oz. can cream of chicken or mushroom soup
- 8-oz. container sour cream
- 3/4 c. mayonnaise
- 2 t. salt
- 1/4 t. pepper
- 8-oz. can water chestnuts, drained and chopped
- 4-oz. mushroom stems & pieces, drained
- 3 stalks celery, chopped
- 1 T. onion, finely chopped
- 1/4 c. shredded Cheddar cheese
- 3/4 c. club crackers, crushed
- 3 T. butter, melted
- 1/2 c. sliced almonds

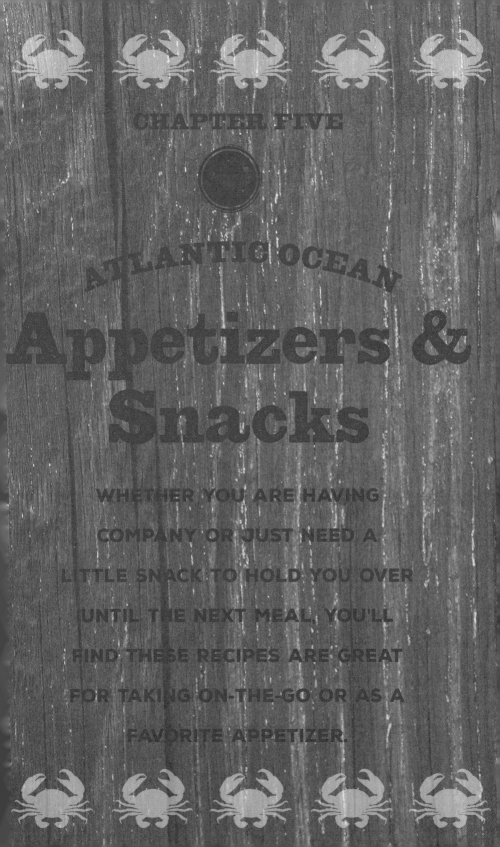

CHAPTER FIVE

ATLANTIC OCEAN

Appetizers & Snacks

WHETHER YOU ARE HAVING

COMPANY OR JUST NEED A

LITTLE SNACK TO HOLD YOU OVER

UNTIL THE NEXT MEAL, YOU'LL

FIND THESE RECIPES ARE GREAT

FOR TAKING ON-THE-GO OR AS A

FAVORITE APPETIZER.

ROQUEFORT CUT-OUT CRACKERS

LINDA HENDERSON
SUNSET, NC

I like to choose cookie cutters in shapes to match the occasion.

1 c. all-purpose flour
7 T. crumbled Roquefort or blue cheese
1 egg yolk
4 t. whipping cream
7 T. butter, softened
1/8 t. salt
cayenne pepper to taste
1/2 t. dried parsley

Stir together all ingredients in a large bowl until dough forms. Cover; let stand for 30 minutes. On a floured surface, roll out dough to 1/8-inch thickness. Cut out dough with a round cookie cutter or other desired shape; arrange on an ungreased baking sheet. Bake at 400 degrees for 7 to 9 minutes, just until golden. Let cool on baking sheet; store in an airtight container.

Makes 2 dozen.

NACHO CHICKEN DIP

TRUDY WILLIAMS
MIDDLESEX, NC

We love this delicious dip at parties...it's even good as a meal, paired with a side salad.

16-oz. can refried beans
12-oz. can chicken, drained
16-oz. jar chunky salsa
8-oz. pkg. shredded Mexican-blend cheese
tortilla chips

Layer beans, chicken, salsa and cheese in a lightly greased one-quart casserole dish. Bake, uncovered, at 350 degrees for 30 minutes, or until cheese is bubbly. Serve hot with tortilla chips.

Makes about 6-1/2 cups.

SANDWICH ON A STICK

AMY THOMASON HUNT
TRAPHILL, NC

Here's a simple snack to make for a picnic or party. Adjust the quantity and ingredients to suit your family's tastes.

Alternate all ingredients except condiments onto skewers. Garnish as desired.

Makes 8.

1/2 lb. deli ham, cubed
1/2 lb. deli turkey, cubed
1/2 lb. deli chicken, cubed
1/2 lb. Cheddar cheese, cubed
4 c. bread, cubed
1 pt. cherry tomatoes
4 dill pickles, cut into 1-inch pieces
8 wooden skewers
Garnish: mustard, spicy brown mustard, mayonnaise

CANNOLI DIP

AUDRA VANHORN-SOREY
COLUMBIA, NC

A fun spin on a sweet Italian favorite!

In a large bowl, combine cream cheese and butter; blend well. Add powdered sugar; stir well until smooth. Stir in vanilla; fold in chocolate chips. Cover and chill, if not serving immediately. Serve with graham crackers or vanilla wafers.

Makes 10 servings.

8-oz. pkg. cream cheese, softened
1/2 c. butter, softened
3/4 c. powdered sugar
1/2 t. vanilla extract
1 c. mini semi-sweet chocolate chips
plain or cinnamon graham crackers or vanilla wafers

CURRY VEGETABLE DIP

**LYNNETTE JONES
EAST FLAT ROCK, NC**

*I have made this simple recipe for quite some time and it is always a
favorite. Be sure to allow time for it to chill to blend the flavors together.
Serve with your favorite sliced fresh vegetables.*

1 c. mayonnaise
1 t. onion, grated
1 t. prepared
   horseradish
1/2 t. curry powder
1 t. white vinegar

Combine all ingredients in a bowl; mix well. Cover
and refrigerate for 4 hours to overnight to allow
flavors to blend.

Makes 15 servings.

MINI CHICKEN CAESAR CUPS

**MIA ROSSI
CHARLOTTE, NC**

*Tasty little morsels that my guests love! I like to prep the filling and press
the biscuits into the muffin tin a bit ahead of time. Then it's a snap to bake
and fill at party time.*

12-oz. tube refrigerated
   flaky biscuits
1 c. cooked chicken,
   finely chopped
3 T. Caesar salad
   dressing
1/4 c. romaine lettuce,
   finely sliced
1/4 c. shredded
   Parmesan cheese

Separate biscuits; split each biscuit into 2 layers.
Press biscuit pieces into 20 ungreased mini muffin
cups; dough should extend 1/4 inch above cups.
In a small bowl, mix chicken and dressing. Spoon
2 teaspoons of mixture into each cup. Bake at 400
degrees for 8 to 11 minutes, until crust is deeply
golden. Remove from muffin tin; top with lettuce and
cheese. Serve warm.

Makes 20 pieces.

WARM CHEESY SPINACH DIP

TINA BARBOUR
LEASBURG, NC

In the summer, Saturday night get-togethers are a routine at our house. When the sun begins to set, the kids head inside to watch movies or play games and the grown-ups head outside to have a drink and unwind from the week. Instead of a heavy meal, we have an appetizer potluck. This spinach dip is my go-to dish!

Combine spinach, cream cheese, seasonings and 1-1/2 cups shredded cheese in a large bowl. Stir until completely blended. Spoon mixture into a lightly greased 8"x8" baking pan or 9" pie plate. Smooth out top; top with remaining cheese. Bake, uncovered, at 350 degrees for 15 minutes, or until heated through and edges are lightly golden. Serve with tortilla chips.

Serves 10 to 12.

10-oz. pkg. frozen chopped spinach, thawed and pressed dry
2 8-oz. pkgs. cream cheese, softened
1 t. onion powder
1 t. salt
1 t. pepper
8-oz. pkg. shredded mozzarella or Italian-blend cheese, divided
tortilla chips

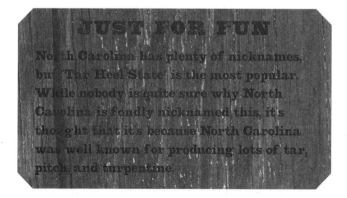

JUST FOR FUN

North Carolina has plenty of nicknames, but "Tar Heel State" is the most popular. While nobody is quite sure why North Carolina is fondly nicknamed this, it's thought that it's because North Carolina was well known for producing lots of tar, pitch, and turpentine.

BOO'S PIMENTO CHEESE

ABBY KRAMER
ASHEVILLE, NC

My grandfather is known as Boo. He is now 80 years old and still makes this dip to bring along whenever he comes to visit. It's the best pimento cheese I've ever tasted, and it's versatile too! It can be warmed and served as a hot cheese dip with tortilla chips or dolloped onto grilled steaks. We even like to make grilled pimento cheese sandwiches with it. Try it...you'll love it too!

3/4 lb. extra-sharp **New York Cheddar cheese**

1 lb. **Colby or Longhorn cheese**

2-oz. jar diced pimentos, drained

assorted crackers

Put cheeses into a food processor. Process until cheese starts to clump, stopping before a smooth texture is reached. Transfer cheese mixture to a large bowl and stir in pimentos. Serve with crackers.

Makes 6 servings.

MINI FRUIT TARTS WITH BRIE

KRISTIN TURNER
RALEIGH, NC

These sweet little treats are fun to whip up for a party! Strawberry, raspberry, peach and apricot preserves as well as orange marmalade all work well, so use your favorites. I like to mix & match and offer a variety of flavors.

2 2.1-oz. pkg's. frozen **mini phyllo cups**

1 c. white chocolate chips

1/4 lb. **Brie cheese, cut into 1/2-inch cubes**

3/4 c. favorite-flavor fruit preserves

Assemble frozen phyllo cups on a non-stick baking sheet. Fill each cup with 2 to 3 white chocolate chips, one cheese cube and one teaspoon preserves. Bake at 350 degrees for about 9 minutes, until warmed through. Serve warm or at room temperature, garnished with several more chocolate chips, if desired.

Makes 2-1/2 dozen.

CRANBERRY JEZEBEL SAUCE

ZOE BENNETT
COLUMBIA, SC

We love this sassy sauce with a holiday twist! Spoon it over cream cheese and serve with crackers for an easy appetizer.

Combine water and sugars in a saucepan. Stir well; bring to a boil over medium heat. Add cranberries. Return to a boil; cook for 10 minutes, stirring occasionally. Spoon into a bowl; cool to room temperature. Stir in horseradish and mustard; cover and chill.

Makes about 2-1/2 cups.

1 c. water
1/2 c. sugar
1/2 c. brown sugar, packed
12-oz. pkg. fresh cranberries
3 T. prepared horseradish
1 T. Dijon mustard

BACON CHEESEBURGER DIP

AMY THOMASON HUNT
TRAPHILL, NC

All the tastes of a great cheeseburger in one tasty dip!

Reserve 2 tablespoons bacon bits; set aside. In a large skillet over medium heat, brown beef or turkey; drain. Reduce heat to low and stir in cheeses and tomatoes with juice. Cook and stir until heated through. Pour mixture into a 2-quart slow cooker. Cover and cook on low setting for 2 to 3 hours. Before serving, stir in parsley and sprinkle with reserved bacon bits. Serve with assorted dippers.

Serves 10 to 12.

6-oz. pkg. real bacon bits, divided
1/2 lb. lean ground beef or turkey
8-oz. pkg. cream cheese, cubed
2 c. shredded Cheddar cheese
10-oz. can diced tomatoes with green chiles
1 t. dried parsley
assorted dippers, such as mini bagel chips, tortilla chips and sliced green and red peppers

SPINACH & FETA TURNOVERS

ROBIN LAZARO
GARNER, NC

This is a family favorite I've perfected over the years. Everyone loves these turnovers, and they're easy to make.

2 T. olive oil
1/4 c. onion, chopped
1 to 2 cloves garlic, minced
10-oz. pkg. frozen spinach, thawed and well drained
1/4 c. sour cream
1/8 t. nutmeg
salt and pepper to taste
1/2 c. crumbled feta cheese
Optional: 1/2 c. cooked chicken, shredded
8-oz. tube refrigerated crescent rolls
1 egg white, beaten

Heat olive oil in a skillet over medium heat. Add onion and garlic; cook and stir until translucent. Stir in spinach, sour cream and seasonings; remove from heat. Add cheese and chicken, if using; set aside. Separate crescent rolls, leaving each 2 triangles attached to form 4 squares. Press perforations to seal. Add 2 tablespoons spinach mixture to one half of each square. Fold over; seal edges with a fork. Place turnovers on an ungreased baking sheet. Bake at 350 degrees for 20 to 30 minutes, until golden.

Makes 4 servings.

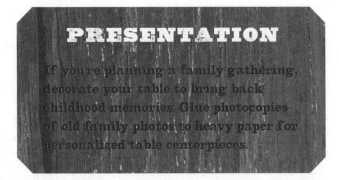

PRESENTATION

If you're planning a family gathering, decorate your table to bring back childhood memories. Glue photocopies of old family photos to heavy paper for personalized table centerpieces.

UPCOUNTRY PARTY SPREAD

**RALICE GERTZ
GREENSBORO, NC**

This recipe was given to me by a dear friend about 8 years ago. It's still a favorite!

Combine all ingredients except crackers in a medium bowl; mix well. Serve with crackers.

Makes 15 servings.

6 slices bacon, crisply cooked and crumbled
1 c. shredded sharp Cheddar cheese
1 c. grated Parmesan Cheese
1 c. mayonnaise
1/4 c. onion, finely chopped
1/8 t. garlic powder
2-oz. pkg. slivered almonds
assorted crackers

3-PEPPER CHICKEN BITES

**AMY BRADSHER
ROXBORO, NC**

This is such a fun appetizer for a party! Sweet with a kick, it can be tossed together quickly and ready for the oven when your guests arrive. How can you go wrong with bacon?

Cut bacon slices in thirds. Wrap each piece of chicken with a strip of bacon and fasten with a wooden toothpick; set aside. Mix together remaining ingredients in a small bowl. Dredge each piece in brown sugar mixture. Place on a wire rack on an aluminum foil-lined baking sheet. Bake at 350 degrees for 30 to 35 minutes, until chicken juices run clear and bacon is crisp.

Makes 2 to 2-1/2 dozen.

1/2 lb. bacon
1 lb. boneless, skinless chicken breasts, cut into one-inch cubes
2/3 c. brown sugar, packed
1 t. cayenne pepper
1 t. chili powder
1/8 t. pepper

 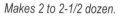

CANDY SPRINKLES CHEESECAKE BALL

AUDRA VANHORN-SOREY
COLUMBIA, NC

A sweet and easy treat that's a birthday cake lover's dream!

8-oz. pkg cream cheese, softened
1/2 c. butter, softened
1-1/2 c. cake mix with candy sprinkles
1/2 c. powdered sugar
3 T. sugar
1/2 c. rainbow candy sprinkles
vanilla wafers, graham crackers

In a large bowl, beat cream cheese and butter together until combined. Add dry cake mix and sugars; stir until combined. Scoop mixture onto a large piece of plastic wrap; form into a ball. Wrap and freeze for 90 minutes, or until firm enough to hold its shape. Pour candy sprinkles into a bowl. Unwrap cheese ball; roll in sprinkles until completely covered. Place on a serving dish; serve with vanilla wafers or graham crackers.

Serves 12 to 20.

KITCHEN TIP

A fondue pot is a must for keeping sweet & savory dips just right for serving. Simply fill the fondue pot, turn it to the warm setting and forget about it!

CHEESY SAUSAGE DIP

EMILY JORDAN
SOPHIA, NC

One year for Christmas, my mom made me a cookbook with recipes from my great-great-grandmas, great-grandmas, grandmas, distant relatives, aunts and even my uncle. The book is a treasure and I love it dearly. This recipe was shared by my dad's cousin Lisa. It's a staple when my best friends and I get together for a sleepover or for movie night.

Brown sausage in a skillet over medium heat; drain. Place sausage in a slow cooker. Add cheese. Pour salsa over top. Cover and cook on low setting for 1-1/2 to 2 hours. Serve with tortilla chips or party rye bread.

Serves 8 to 10.

1 lb. ground pork sausage
16-oz. pkg. pasteurized process cheese spread, cubed
1-1/4 c. salsa
tortilla chips, sliced
party rye bread

STICKS & STONES

JEWEL SHARPE
RALEIGH, NC

A delicious and festive party appetizer...there are never any leftovers at our get-togethers!

Add sausage and meatballs to a slow cooker. In a microwave-safe bowl, combine jellies and mustard; microwave on high setting until mixture is melted and well blended. Pour hot jelly mixture over kielbasa and meatballs. Cover and cook on low setting for one to 2 hours, until heated through. Serve with pretzel sticks or toothpicks.

Serves 12 to 16.

14-oz. Kielbasa sausage ring, cut into bite-size pieces
32-oz. pkg. frozen mini meatballs, thawed
10-oz. jar currant jelly
10-oz. jar red pepper jelly
1 T. Dijon mustard
pretzel sticks or toothpicks

EASY PEANUT WONTONS

YVONNE COLEMAN
STATESVILLE, NC

I came up with this recipe one day when I was in the mood for wontons. I'm not a big fan of cabbage, so I went to the kitchen and played with some ingredients I had on hand. I chose four of my favorites and added soy sauce and sugar. Yum!

1 c. carrots, peeled and shredded

1 c. zucchini, shredded

1 c. peanuts, finely ground

1 c. mushrooms, finely chopped

1/2 t. sugar

3 T. light soy sauce

16-oz. pkg. wonton wrappers

oil for deep frying

12-oz. bottle sweet-and-sour sauce or duck sauce

Mix together carrots, zucchini, peanuts, mushrooms, sugar and soy sauce in a medium bowl. Mixture should be slightly moist and stick together. Place one tablespoon mixture near the center of each wonton wrapper. Fold wrappers according to package directions. Moisten ends of wrappers and roll to seal. In a deep fryer, heat oil to 3-inch depth. Drop wontons, one at a time, into hot oil; fry for approximately 2 to 3 minutes, turning until golden. Remove from oil; drain on paper towels. Serve warm with desired sauce.

Makes about 2 dozen.

MAPLEY APPETIZERS

LYNNETTE JONES
EAST FLAT ROCK, NC

With traditional Christmas colors from the green pepper and the red maraschino cherries, this is a wonderful holiday appetizer. The recipe was passed down to me by my husband's aunt.

In a bowl, blend reserved pineapple juice, maple syrup, vinegar and water; stir in cornstarch. Pour into a slow cooker. Add pineapple and remaining ingredients; stir gently. Cover and cook on low setting for 4 to 6 hours.

Serves 8 to 10.

15-1/4 oz. can pineapple
    tidbits, drained and
    juice reserved
1/2 c. maple syrup
1/2 c. vinegar
1/3 c. water
4 t. cornstarch
14-oz. pkg. mini smoked
    sausages
2/3 c. green pepper, cut
    into 1" squares
1/2 c. maraschino
    cherries

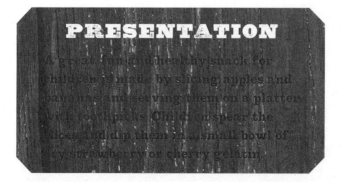

PRESENTATION

A great fun and healthy snack for children is made by slicing apples and bananas and serving them on a platter with toothpicks. Children spear the slices and dip them in a small bowl of dry strawberry or cherry gelatin.

CHAPTER SIX

TAR HEEL

Treats & Sweets

THERE IS ALWAYS ROOM FOR
DESSERT, SO WHEN YOUR SWEET
TOOTH IS CALLING, THESE SIMPLE
SWEETS ARE THE PERFECT WAY TO
END THE DAY.

CREAM CHEESE POUND CAKE

WANDA PARDUE FOSTER
WILKESBORO, NC

This cake won two blue ribbons for me at the county fair! I like to blend the butter and sugar with my hands...it results in a better cake.

1 c. all-purpose flour
18-1/2 oz. pkg. yellow
  butter cake mix
1/2 c. butter, softened
1 c. sugar
4 eggs
8-oz. pkg. cream cheese,
  softened
1/2 t. vanilla extract
1 c. milk

Combine flour and dry cake mix in a bowl; set aside. In a separate bowl, blend together butter and sugar until very creamy. Add eggs, one at a time, mixing well; add cream cheese and vanilla. Alternately add flour mixture and milk to butter mixture, starting and ending with flour mixture. Pour batter into a greased and floured tube pan. Place pan in a cold oven; turn oven to 325 degrees. Bake for one hour, or until cake tests done with a toothpick.

Serves 12 to 14.

BROWN SUGAR PUDDIN' PIES

ANGELA NICHOLS
MOUNT AIRY, NC

Bite-size, brown sugar pies...great for any get-together.

15-ct. pkg. frozen mini
  phyllo cups, unbaked
1/2 c. butter, softened
3/4 c. sugar
3/4 c. brown sugar,
  packed
2 eggs, beaten
1/2 c. half-and-half
1/2 t. vanilla extract
Garnish: whipped
  topping and nutmeg

Bake mini cups on an ungreased baking sheet at 350 degrees for 4 to 5 minutes; set aside. Beat butter and sugars together until light and fluffy; blend in eggs, half-and-half and vanilla. Spoon into cups; sprinkle tops with nutmeg. Bake at 350 degrees for 15 to 20 minutes, until set. Top with a dollop of whipped topping and a dusting of nutmeg before serving.

Makes 15 servings.

EASY APPLE PIE COOKIE BARS

AUDRA VANHORN-SOREY
COLUMBIA, NC

A family favorite...so easy, the kids can help pat out the dough!

Press 2/3 of cookie dough into the bottom of a greased 9"x9" baking pan. Combine sugar and cinnamon in a small bowl; sprinkle 2/3 of mixture evenly over dough. Spread pie filling over dough. Take small amounts of remaining cookie dough, flatten slightly and place over the pie filling. Do not cover filling completely. Sprinkle with remaining cinnamon-sugar. Bake at 350 degrees for 30 minutes, or until cookie crust is done. Cool completely before cutting.

Makes 12 servings.

16-1/2 oz. tube refrigerated sugar cookie dough, divided
1/4 c. sugar
4 t. cinnamon
21-oz. can apple pie filling

S'MORES COBBLER

AUDRA VANHORN-SOREY
COLUMBIA, NC

A unique twist on a family favorite...it's sure to be a hit!

Prepare pudding mix with milk according to package directions; cool slightly. Spoon pudding into an ungreased 13"x9" baking pan. Arrange graham crackers over pudding, with some space between crackers. Sprinkle with chocolate chips; spread dry cake mix over top and dot with butter. Bake at 350 degrees for 25 minutes. Remove from oven; stir slightly to ensure all ingredients are moistened. Top with marshmallows. Bake for an additional 8 to 10 minutes, until marshmallows are melted.

Makes 10 servings.

5-oz. pkg. cook & serve chocolate pudding mix
1 c. whole milk
6 whole graham crackers, broken in half
1/2 c. mini semi-sweet chocolate chips
18-1/2 oz. pkg. chocolate cake mix
1/2 c. butter, sliced
10-oz. pkg. marshmallows

FORGET 'EM COOKIES

GLENDA ANDERSON
LOUISBURG, NC

My mom made these cookies for my sister and me when we were little. When you bite into a cookie, it melts in your mouth! When I got old enough to bake by myself, I started making these cookies for Thanksgiving and Christmas.

2 egg whites
2/3 c. sugar
1/8 t. salt
1 t. vanilla extract
1 c. mini semi-sweet chocolate chips
1 c. chopped pecans

Preheat oven to 350 degrees. In a deep bowl, beat egg whites with an electric mixer on high speed until stiff peaks form. Gradually add sugar and salt; beat well. Add vanilla and mix thoroughly. Fold in chocolate chips and pecans with a spoon. Drop mixture by teaspoonfuls onto parchment paper-lined baking sheets, 2 inches apart. Place pans in preheated oven; turn off the heat. Leave in oven at least 3 hours or overnight before removing.

Makes 3 dozen.

LUSCIOUS PEACH ICE CREAM

NANCY GRADY WILSON
KENANSVILLE, NC

I've always savored the flavor of homemade peach ice cream... waiting expectantly, watching the transformation and celebrating the miracle with family & friends. Elberta and Georgia Bell peaches are excellent varieties to use. Enjoy!

2 c. peaches, halved, pitted and cut up
3 c. sugar, divided
juice of 1/2 lemon
4 eggs, lightly beaten
3 T. self-rising flour
1/8 t. salt
5 c. whole milk
2 c. whipping cream

Purée peaches in a blender. Mix in one cup sugar and lemon juice; refrigerate mixture until chilled. In a bowl, whisk together eggs, remaining sugar, flour and salt. Heat milk just to boiling; cool slightly. Pour egg mixture into the top of a double boiler. Slowly add milk to egg mixture. Cook over medium heat until thickened, stirring frequently. Cool. Combine peaches, egg mixture and cream in an ice cream freezer, stirring to blend all ingredients. Freeze according to manufacturer's directions.

Makes about 4 quarts.

  - - - - -

GOOD-FOR-YOU CHOCOLATE CHIP COOKIES

KACIE DAMME
PINEVILLE, NC

Wanting to find a satisfying, healthy cookie packed with flavor and good nutrition, I created this recipe. My husband loves chocolate chip cookies, and now he prefers these cookies! They hold up well in cookie jars and lunchboxes too.

With an electric mixer on medium speed, beat together brown sugar, butter and butter blend. Beat in eggs and vanilla. Add remaining ingredients all at once except oats and chocolate chips. Stir until combined. Beat with an electric mixer on medium speed for one to 2 minutes, until well blended. Fold in oats and chocolate chips with a spoon, just until mixed. Drop by tablespoonfuls onto lightly greased baking sheets. Flatten cookies slightly. Bake at 350 degrees for 8 to 10 minutes, until golden. Let cool 2 to 3 minutes on baking sheets before transferring to a wire rack.

Makes about 6 dozen.

2 c. brown sugar, packed
1/2 c. butter, softened
1/2 c. 50/50 butter blend
2 eggs, beaten
1 t. vanilla extract
2-1/4 c. whole-wheat flour
1/4 c. wheat germ
1/2 t. salt
1 t. baking soda
1/8 t. cinnamon
Optional: 3 T. golden flaxseed
2 c. quick-cooking oats, uncooked
1 c. semi-sweet chocolate chips

POTATO CHIP COOKIES

CYNTHIA MANGUM
CREEDMOOR, NC

This recipe is requested every Christmas. People who have never tried it are always amazed that a cookie with potato chips in it can taste so good!

1 c. shortening
1 c. sugar
1 c. brown sugar, packed
2 eggs, beaten
1 t. vanilla extract
2 c. all-purpose flour
1 t. baking soda
1/2 t. salt
2 c. potato chips, crushed
1/2 c. chopped peanuts

Blend together shortening and sugars. Beat in eggs and vanilla; set aside. In a separate bowl, sift together flour, baking soda and salt. Add our mixture to shortening mixture. Mix well; stir in remaining ingredients. Drop by teaspoonfuls onto lightly greased baking sheets. Bake at 350 degrees for 10 to 12 minutes, until edges are golden. Let cool on baking sheets for 2 minutes; remove to a wire rack and cool completely.

Makes 2 to 3 dozen.

MORAVIAN COOKIES

PATTI WALKER
MOCKSVILLE, NC

When I was growing up, Christmas at our house meant making wafer-thin, crisp, spicy Moravian cookies. Mom put the ingredients in the big bowl and allowed me to "smush" it all together. Then my mom, grandmother, sister and I would roll out the chilled dough as thin as possible and cut it with cookie cutters. It was messy, but so much fun! I do this with my own children now and they enjoy the tradition as much as I do.

In a very large bowl, blend shortening and sugar together. Add spices and baking soda. Slowly add molasses, alternating with flour. Mix very well, using either your hands or a stand mixer. Cover and chill dough for several hours, until firm. Dough may be kept refrigerated or frozen for several weeks and thawed when ready to bake. Working with a small amount of dough at a time, roll out 1/8-inch thick on a floured surface. Cut out with desired cookie cutters. Place on ungreased baking sheets. Bake at 375 degrees for 5 to 6 minutes, watching carefully, until golden. Allow cookies to cool completely on baking sheets.

Makes about 12 dozen.

2-1/3 c. shortening

2-1/4 c. brown sugar, packed

1/4 c. ground ginger

1/4 c. ground cloves

1/4 c. cinnamon

2 T. baking soda

4 c. dark molasses

20 c. all-purpose flour, sifted

KITCHEN TIP

A fragrant cup of cinnamon coffee is the perfect partner for Old-Fashioned Applesauce Cake. Just add a teaspoon of cinnamon and 1/4 cup of brown sugar to the coffeepot before brewing.

GRANDMA'S JELLY COOKIES

PAM MCCOURT
MARLBORO, NC

This simple recipe has been used in our family for four generations. I'm happy to have it in my grandmother's handwriting. My mother made these cookies often, so they bring back memories of my childhood. We used to enjoy them for dessert, warm from the oven. They are easy to put together.

1 c. shortening
1 c. sugar
2 eggs, beaten
1 t. vanilla extract
2-3/4 c. all-purpose flour
1/4 c. favorite jelly or
   jam

In a large bowl, mix together shortening, sugar, eggs and vanilla. Stir in flour. Roll into one-inch balls; place on ungreased baking sheets. Using your thumb, press an indent gently in the middle of each cookie. Fill with 1/2 teaspoon jelly or jam. Bake at 375 degrees for 10 to 15 minutes, until golden on the edges.

Makes 2 dozen.

VIVIAN'S PRUNE CAKE

**DEBBIE MULLIS
CONCORD, NC**

*My mom has made this cake for over 50 years. It is a very moist spicy
cake with chocolate icing...and you know, everything tastes better with
chocolate! She would bake a cake on Saturday and it would not be cut
until Sunday and as long as it lasted, you enjoyed cake all week.*

Cover dried prunes with water in a medium
saucepan. Simmer over low heat until soft, about
30 minutes. Drain prunes, reserving one cup liquid;
mash with a potato masher and set aside. With an
electric mixer on medium speed, beat eggs and
sugar together; mix in butter, prunes and reserved
liquid. Add flour, baking soda, salt and spices; mix
well. Pour batter into 3 greased and floured 9"
round cake pans. Bake at 350 degrees for 20 to 30
minutes. Cool; assemble with Chocolate Icing.

Chocolate Icing:

Melt butter in a saucepan over low heat; add cocoa
and vanilla. Stir in powdered sugar. If too thick, add
milk to right consistency.

Serves 10 to 12.

16-oz. pkg. dried pitted
  prunes
4 eggs
2 c. sugar
1/4 c. butter, softened
2 c. all-purpose flour
2 t. baking soda
1/8 t. salt
1 t. cinnamon
1 t. ground cloves
1 t. nutmeg

CHOCOLATE ICING
1/2 c. butter
1/4 c. baking cocoa
1 t. vanilla extract
16-oz. pkg. powdered
  sugar
Optional: 1 to 3 T.
  evaporated milk

GRANDMA BATCHELOR'S CHOCOLATE ROLL

SUE ROSA
NEW BERN, NC

Grandma Batchelor always had a big family gathering at Christmastime with lots of home-baked goodies. Her chocolate roll was a special favorite that still brings back some of my best childhood memories. These are so easy to make that I usually make 6 to 12 rolls to give as gifts!

1 c. cake flour
1 t. baking powder
1/4 t. salt
2 T. margarine, melted
1/3 c. hot water
4 eggs
1 c. sugar
1/2 t. vanilla extract
Optional: powdered
sugar

CHOCOLATE SYRUP
1-1/2 c. sugar
1/2 c. water
7 to 8 T. baking cocoa

Sift together cake flour, baking powder and salt; set aside. Combine margarine and hot water in a cup; let cool slightly. Beat eggs in a separate large bowl, gradually adding sugar and vanilla. Add margarine mixture to egg mixture, beating slowly. Slowly add flour mixture until smooth; batter will be very thin. Pour evenly into a wax paper-lined 15"x10" jelly-roll pan. Bake at 400 degrees for about 15 minutes, until lightly golden. Invert hot cake onto a tea towel. Peel off wax paper; trim edges all around cake. Roll cake up in tea towel and let cool. Unroll cake. Spread Chocolate Syrup over cake, adding as much or as little as desired. Allow syrup to soak into the cake; roll cake into a log. Sprinkle with powdered sugar, if desired.

Chocolate Syrup:

Heat ingredients to a boil, stirring constantly. Cool slightly.

Makes 12 to 15 servings.

STRAWBERRY-RHUBARB PIE

SHAR TOLIVER
LILLINGTON, NC

After our family relocated to North Carolina where strawberries are plentiful, I decided to make a pie using the best of what is grown locally and this is the result. The combination of a sweet crust with a tart filling is the perfect taste of summer.

Combine strawberries and rhubarb; set aside. Sift together sugars, flour, cornstarch, salt and cinnamon. Stir into strawberry mixture. Place crust in a 9" pie plate; chill for 10 minutes. Spoon strawberry mixture into crust; dot with butter. Sprinkle Crumb Topping over filling. Bake at 400 degrees for 50 to 60 minutes, or until topping is golden. Set pie on a wire rack to cool for 2 hours.

Crumb Topping:

Mix together flour, sugar and salt; cut in butter until crumbly.

Makes 8 servings.

5 c. strawberries, hulled and chopped
2 stalks rhubarb, peeled and diced
3/4 c. brown sugar, packed
1/2 c. sugar
1/4 c. all-purpose flour
2 T. cornstarch
1/8 t. salt
1/2 t. cinnamon
9-inch pie crust
1-1/2 T. butter, diced

CRUMB TOPPING
3 T. all-purpose flour
1/8 t. salt
1 T. sugar
1 T. butter, softened

MARTHA'S SHREDDED APPLE PIE

PATTI WALKER
MOCKSVILLE, NC

Every year at Christmastime, my Grandmother Martha would make the best apple pies. The first time my boyfriend tasted her pie, he said he would definitely marry me if I could cook as well as she did. I guess I passed the test, because we have been married many years! This is a family heirloom recipe that my Granny (great-grandmother) first made... don't tell my grandmother I shared it!

8 Granny Smith apples, cored, peeled and shredded
1/4 t. lemon juice
1-1/2 t. apple pie spice
2 9-inch pie crusts
1/2 c. butter, melted
2 c. sugar
3 eggs, beaten
nutmeg to taste

Place apples in a large bowl; toss with lemon juice and spice. Pierce unbaked crusts lightly with a fork; fill with apples. Mix melted butter, sugar and eggs; pour mixture evenly over apples. Dust the top of each pie with a dash of nutmeg. Bake at 350 degrees for 45 minutes to an hour. Allow to cool (if you can wait!) before slicing.

Makes 2 pies, 6 servings each.

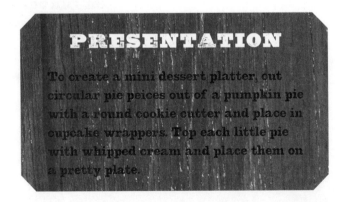

PRESENTATION

To create a mini dessert platter, cut circular pie peices out of a pumpkin pie with a round cookie cutter and place in cupcake wrappers. Top each little pie with whipped cream and place them on a pretty plate.

PEANUT BUTTER BROWNIE TRIFLE

LYNNETTE JONES
EAST FLAT ROCK, NC

This really feeds a lot of folks! It's a good dessert to make if you are having company.

Prepare and bake brownies according to package directions. Cool completely in pan on a wire rack. Cut brownies into one-inch cubes; set aside. Combine milk and pudding mix in a large bowl. Beat with an electric mixer on medium speed for 2 minutes. Cover and refrigerate for 10 to 15 minutes. Fold vanilla, peanut butter and 1-1/2 cups whipped topping into pudding; set aside. Cut peanut butter cups into 4 pieces each. In a large clear glass trifle bowl, layer 1/3 each of brownie cubes and pudding; add 1/4 of peanut butter cups. Repeat layering twice. Spread with remaining topping; garnish with remaining peanut butter cups. Cover and chill until serving time.

Serves 12 to 14.

18-oz. pkg. brownie mix

3 c. milk

5.1-oz. pkg. instant vanilla pudding mix

2 t. vanilla extract

1/2 c. creamy peanut butter

2 c. frozen whipped topping, thawed

1-1/2 12-oz. pkg's. mini peanut butter cups

SPECIAL STRAWBERRY PIE

WENDY CARVER
WAYNESVILLE, NC

My sweet grandpa is diabetic, but even diabetics can get a sweet tooth every now and then! I hated seeing him left out of dessert at family gatherings so I tweaked this strawberry pie until I had something he could enjoy too! Now my family likes it so much, I usually make this version instead of the real thing.

1 c. diet lemon-lime soda

3-oz. pkg. sugar-free strawberry gelatin mix

1 T. cornstarch

3 c. strawberries, hulled and sliced

1 to 2 pkts. calorie-free powdered sweetener

9-inch pie crust, baked

In a small saucepan over medium heat, combine soda, gelatin mix and cornstarch. Cook and stir over medium heat until slightly thickened. Add strawberries; bring to a boil. Cool completely; stir in desired amount of sweetener. Spoon into baked crust; cover and chill until set.

Serves 8.

ICE CREAM SANDWICH DESSERT

ANN CRANE
PLEASANT GARDEN, NC

This yummy recipe was given to me by my friend Doris. She's one of the best cooks I know. It's like an ice cream sundae...only sliced and eaten like a cake.

Place 12 ice cream sandwiches in a single layer in a 13"x11" aluminum foil baking pan. Spread half of whipped topping over sandwiches. Drizzle pineapple or strawberry topping over whipped topping. Place remaining sandwiches on top; spread with remaining whipped topping. Garnish with caramel topping, chocolate syrup, nuts and cherries. Freeze until serving. Cut into squares.

Serves 24 to 28.

24 ice cream sandwiches, unwrapped

16-oz. container frozen whipped topping, thawed

1/3 to 1/2 c. pineapple or strawberry ice cream topping

Garnish: caramel topping, chocolate syrup, chopped nuts, maraschino cherries

JUST FOR FUN

He might have been born in Baltimore, but iconic baseball player Babe Ruth made history in Fayetteville, North Carolina on March 7, 1914, when he hit his first professional home run.

PUMPKIN CREAM CHEESE MUFFINS

CONNIE BAILEY
ADVANCE, NC

*My grandchild loves these special muffins for breakfast year 'round.
The staff at the vet's office where my husband works love them too.*

3-1/2 c. all-purpose flour
3 c. sugar
2 t. baking soda
1 t. cinnamon
1 t. salt
2 c. canned pumpkin
4 eggs, beaten
2/3 c. water
1 c. oil

CREAM CHEESE FILLING
1-1/2 c. cream cheese, softened
1/2 c. sugar
1 egg, beaten
1/8 t. salt, divided

In a large bowl, combine flour, sugar, baking soda, cinnamon and salt. Mix well and set aside. In another bowl, beat remaining ingredients until blended. Add pumpkin mixture to flour mixture; stir well until blended. To each of 18 paper-lined muffin cups, add 2 tablespoons batter, one tablespoon Cream Cheese Filling and another 2 tablespoons batter. Bake at 350 degrees for 20 minutes, or until set. Cool on a wire rack.

Cream Cheese Filling:

Combine all ingredients in a large bowl; beat until blended well.

Makes 1-1/2 dozen.

BROWNIE-STUFFED CHOCOLATE CHIP COOKIES

KRISTIN TURNER
FUQUAY-VARINA, NC

This is a perfect recipe for cookie exchanges. I mean, a chocolate chip cookie that's been stuffed with a brownie? It's two of the best desserts in one!

Prepare brownie mix according to package directions; bake in an 8"x8" baking pan. Cool completely; cut into one-inch squares. In a bowl, beat together butter and shortening with an electric mixer on medium speed until creamy. Add brown sugar to butter mixture; beat until smooth. Add eggs, egg yolk and vanilla; beat until blended. In a separate bowl, sift together flour, baking powder, baking soda and salt. Gradually beat flour mixture into butter mixture until well combined. Fold in chocolate chips. Cover and refrigerate dough for one hour. For each cookie, enclose a brownie square in 1/2 cup cookie dough. Place cookies on parchment paper-lined baking sheets; chill for 15 minutes. Bake at 350 degrees for 18 to 20 minutes, until golden. Cool on pan for 2 minutes; remove to wire racks to cool completely.

Makes about 11 large cookies.

20-oz. pkg. brownie mix
1/2 c. butter, softened
1/2 c. butter-flavored shortening
1-1/2 c. brown sugar, packed
2 eggs
1 egg yolk
1 T. vanilla extract
2-1/2 c. all-purpose flour
2 t. baking powder
1/2 t. baking soda
1/2 t. salt
3 c. semi-sweet chocolate chips

CINNAMON APPLE COOKIES

DAWN DHOOGHE
CONCORD, NC

Every year my husband, daughter and I go apple picking. We come home with bushels of apples and the baking begins! This is the first recipe I pull out of my tattered box...the recipe that says "fall" to us.

1/2 c. butter, softened
1-1/4 c. brown sugar, packed
1 egg, lightly beaten
2 c. all-purpose flour
1/2 t. baking powder
1/2 t. baking soda
1/4 t. salt
1-1/2 t. cinnamon
1/4 t. nutmeg
1/4 c. milk
1-1/4 c. apples, peeled, cored and diced
1 c. cinnamon baking chips

In a large bowl, with an electric mixer on medium speed, beat butter and brown sugar until light and fluffy. Add egg; beat until blended well and set aside. In another bowl, combine flour, baking powder, baking soda, salt and spices. Add half of flour mixture to butter mixture; stir until mixed well. Add milk; mix well. Fold in apples and baking chips. Drop dough by tablespoonfuls onto lightly greased baking sheets, 2 inches apart. Bake at 375 degrees for 12 to 17 minutes, until cookies start to crust over and a toothpick tests done. Let cookies stand on baking sheets for 5 minutes; remove to a wire rack. Spread Glaze over warm cookies.

Glaze:

Combine powdered sugar, vanilla and enough milk to form a smooth glaze.

Makes 2 dozen.

GLAZE
1-1/2 c. powdered sugar
1 to 2 T. milk
1/2 t. vanilla extract

CREAM CHEESE PUMPKIN SQUARES

PAMELA ELKIN
ASHEVILLE, NC

This recipe is so quick & easy to make that it's one of my favorites to share during the holidays. Be sure to have extra copies of the recipe on hand...everyone will be asking you for it!

Beat cream cheese until fluffy; add condensed milk and beat well. Add 2 beaten eggs, pumpkin and 2 teaspoons spice. Mix well and set aside. Combine dry cake mix, butter and remaining egg and spice. Mix with an electric mixer on low speed until crumbly. Press mixture into the bottom of a greased 13"x9" baking pan to form a crust. Pour cream cheese mixture over crust; sprinkle with nuts. Bake at 350 degrees for 30 to 35 minutes, until set. Chill; cut into squares. Keep refrigerated.

Makes 2 to 3 dozen.

8-oz. pkg. cream cheese, softened
14-oz. can sweetened condensed milk
3 eggs, divided
15-oz. can pumpkin
3 t. pumpkin pie spice, divided
16-oz. pkg. pound cake mix
2 T. butter, melted
1 c. chopped pecans

DINNERTIME CONVERSATION

In 1937, Vernon Rudolph bought a secret recipe from a New Orleans chef and opened a small store in the Winston-Salem area of North Carolina. He started by selling his doughnuts to local grocery stores, and this business eventually turned into the Krispy Kreme people know and love today.

PEANUT BUTTER BALLS

DEANNA MARTINEZ-BEY
WAKE FOREST, NC

This recipe came from my Great-Aunt Mary, and it's very special to me. Every year she would make these at Christmastime and add them to her Christmas cookie platter. I remember digging under all of the other cookies just to find a peanut butter ball!

2 c. chunky peanut butter

1/2 c. butter, room temperature

2 c. powdered sugar

2 c. crispy rice cereal

1 c. milk chocolate chips

8-oz. pkg. semi-sweet baking chocolate, chopped

2 T. paraffin baking wax, chopped

In a large bowl, combine peanut butter, butter, powdered sugar and cereal. Mix well, using your hands; form into one-inch balls. If mixture is too sticky to shape, chill for 30 minutes before rolling. Place balls onto wax paper-lined baking sheets; refrigerate while preparing the coating. Combine remaining ingredients in a double boiler. Cook over hot water until melted; stir until smooth. Using a toothpick or fork, dip balls into chocolate. Return to baking sheets and refrigerate. Keep refrigerated in an airtight container.

Makes 2 to 3 dozen.

NO-BAKE APPLE PIE

DEANNA POLITO-LAUGHINGHOUSE
KNIGHTDALE, NC

The first time I saw this recipe in a very old magazine, I thought it sounded interesting. So I tried it, and it turned out to be one of the best apple pies I ever had! The best part? No oven is required...so it's perfect for summer cooking!

In a large saucepan over medium heat, combine apples, 1-1/2 cups water, dry gelatin mix and spices. Bring to a boil. Reduce heat to low; cover. Simmer for 4 to 6 minutes, until apples are tender. Stir in dry pudding mix and remaining water. Cook and stir for 2 minutes, or until thickened. Remove from heat; fold in nuts. Spoon filling into crust; refrigerate overnight.

Serves 8 to 10.

5 apples, peeled, cored and thinly sliced

1-3/4 c. water, divided

3-oz. pkg. lemon gelatin mix

1/2 t. cinnamon

1/4 t. nutmeg

3-oz. pkg. cook & serve vanilla pudding mix

1/2 c. chopped walnuts

9-inch graham cracker crust

INDEX

Appetizers/Snacks

3-Pepper Chicken Bites, p121
Bacon Cheeseburger Dip, p119
Boo's Pimento Cheese, p118
Candy Sprinkles
   Cheesecake Ball, p122
Cannoli Dip, p115
Cheesy Sausage Dip, p123
Cranberry Jezebel Sauce, p119
Curry Vegetable Dip, p116
Easy Peanut Wontons, p124
Mapley Appetizers, p125
Mini Chicken Caesar Cups, p116
Mini Fruit Tarts with Brie, p118
Nacho Chicken Dip, p114
Roquefort Cut-Out Crackers, p114
Sandwich on a Stick, p115
Spinach & Feta Turnovers, p120
Sticks & Stones, p123
Upcountry Party Spread, p121
Warm Cheesy Spinach Dip, p117

Breads

2-4-1 Drop Biscuits, p43
Beer Bread Biscuits, p48
Carrot Cake Muffins, p50
Diane's Skillet Cornbread, p40
Cheddar Cheese Bread, p40
Crazy-Good Popovers, p39
Creole Cornbread, p39
Harvest Bread, p38
Harvest Pumpkin-Apple
   Bread, p49
Herbed Garlic Bread, p36
Potato Biscuits, p37

Breakfast

Amy's Awesome Sausage
   Ring, p28

Apple & Peanut Butter
   Crescents, p16
Bacon-Egg Cheddar Waffles, p19
Banana-Mango Soy
   Smoothie, p20
Biscuits & Gravy Casserole, p11
Blueberry Buckwheat
   Pancakes, p22
Bran & Raisin Muffins, p8
Breakfast in a Bun, p20
Cherry-Top French Toast, p10
Christmas Morn Sausage
   Bake, p18
Cinnamon-Pecan Sticky Buns, p15
Coconut-Orange Breakfast
   Rolls, p9
Easy Breakfast Strata, p29
Eggs Italiana, p25
Friendship Quiche, p12
Gingerbread Biscuits, p27
Hashbrown Breakfast
   Surprise, p26
Hot Dog Gravy & Biscuits, p17
Make-Ahead Pumpkin Pie French
   Toast, p23
Mixed-Up Ham & Egg Muffins, p14
Nannie's Oatmeal Scones, p25
Peanutty Breakfast Wrap, p16
Pumpkin French Toast Bake, p21
Pumpkin-Caramel Doughnut
   Holes, p47
Smith Family Breakfast Bake, p13
Sweet Twists, p24

Desserts

Brownie-Stuffed Chocolate Chip Cookies, p143

Brown Sugar Puddin' Pies, p128

Cinnamon Apple Cookies, p144

Cream Cheese Pound Cake, p128

Cream Cheese Pumpkin Squares, p145

Easy Apple Pie Cookie Bars, p129

Forget 'Em Cookies, p130

Good-for-You Chocolate Chip Cookies, p131

Grandma Batchelor's Chocolate Roll, p136

Grandma's Jelly Cookies, p134

Ice Cream Sandwich Dessert, p141

Luscious Peach Ice Cream, p130

Martha's Shredded Apple Pie, p138

Moravian Cookies, p133

No-Bake Apple Pie, p147

Peanut Butter Balls, p146

Peanut Butter Brownie Trifle, p139

Potato Chip Cookies, p132

Pumpkin Cream Cheese Muffins, p142

S'mores Cobbler, p129

Special Strawberry Pie, p140

Strawberry-Rhubarb Pie, p137

Vivian's Prune Cake, p135

Mains

Aunt Ruth's Mushroom Chicken, p104

Baked Quesadillas, p80

Balsamic Chicken, p101

Balsamic Chicken & Penne, p99

BBQ Chicken Flatbread, p92

Beef Supper in a Skillet, p109

Buttermilk Fried Chicken, p87

Chicken-Almond Casserole, p111

Chicken Cordon Bleu, p110

Citrus Party Fish, p106

Corn Chip Chicken, p108

Cowgirl Up & Cornbread, p43

Creamy Pesto & Bowties, p92

Easy-Peasy Bolognese Sauce, p103

Garden-To-Table Spinach-Alfredo Pizza, p90

Honey-Mustard Salmon, p95

Lemon Herb & Garlic Shrimp, p98

Lemon-Rice Stuffed Cod & Broccolini, p93

Mandarin Orange Chicken, p102

Mom's Salmon Patties, p91

Pan-Fried Chicken Thighs, p106

Paprika Beef & Noodles, p88

Potluck Pizza Casserole, p107

Roland's Barbecued Spareribs, p100

Rosemary-Garlic Skillet Pork & Potatoes, p104

Shrimp Scampi & Asparagus, p96

Shrimp Soft Tacos, p97

Sloppy Joe Casserole, p78

Spicy Shredded Beef Tostadas, p105

Stuffed Poblano Peppers, p94

Sunday Buttermilk Roast, p95

Tangy BBQ Chicken, p98

Thelma's Pork Chops, p79

Winter Barbecued Chicken, p89

Salads

Audrey's Chicken & Fruit
Salad, p35
Cranberry-Apple Salad, p41
Crunchy Cashew Slaw, p50
Mexican Layered Salad, p34
Mexican Slaw, p42
Wheat Berry & Wild Rice
Salad, p46
Zesty White Bean Salad, p33

Sandwiches

Alberta Prairie Burgers, p64
Almost North Carolina Pulled Pork
BBQ, p58
Beef Eye Roast for
Sandwiches, p69
Egg Salad Sandwiches, p67
Game-Day Sandwich, p55
Grilled Pepper Jack
Sandwiches, p73
Grilled Veggie Sammies, p72
Italian Beef in a Bucket, p73
Mediterranean Sandwiches, p63
Pulled Pork Barbecue, p54
Southern BBQ, p75
Turkey BLT Roll-Ups, p67
Yummy Sloppy Joes, p59

Sides

Amy's 2-Squash Delight, p44
Broccoli-Corn Casserole, p51
Chris's Spicy Mac & Cheese, p32
Cranberry-Apple Bake, p37
Garlicky Savory Parmesan
Asparagus, p36
Hawaiian Asparagus, p33
Herb & Cheese Orzo, p35

Not Your Granny's Brussels
Sprouts, p45
Pineapple Casserole, p32
Ranch Vegetable Bundles, p41
Skillet Potato Pie, p45
Slow-Cooker Beans, p48
Zesty Black-Eyed Peas, p44

Soups

Beefy Macaroni Soup, p62
Carolina Garden Stew, p60
Cheesy Burger Soup, p70
Clam Chowder, p75
Creamy Chicken Chili, p56
Daddy's Corned Beef Soup, p56
Down-Home Split Pea Soup, p74
Easy Taco Soup, p62
Fiesta Corn Chowder, p66
Hearty Fish Chowder, p68
"Mom, It's Good" Chili, p71
Santa Fe Soup, p65
Smoked Sausage-White Bean
Soup, p54
Southwestern Soup, p61
Spicy Corn Chowder with Country
Side Meat, p57

  – – – –

U.S. to METRIC RECIPE EQUIVALENTS

Volume Measurements

¼ teaspoon. 1 mL
½ teaspoon. 2 mL
1 teaspoon . . . . 5 mL
1 tablespoon = 3 teaspoons. . . . . . 15 mL
2 tablespoons = 1 fluid ounce . . . . 30 mL
¼ cup. . . . . 60 mL
⅓ cup. . . . . 75 mL
½ cup = 4 fluid ounces. . . . . 125 mL
1 cup = 8 fluid ounces . . . . 250 mL
2 cups = 1 pint = 16 fluid ounces 500 mL
4 cups = 1 quart . . . . 1 L

Weights

1 ounce . . . . 30 g
4 ounces . . . . 120 g
8 ounces . . . . 225 g
16 ounces = 1 pound . . . . 450 g

Baking Pan Sizes
Square
8x8x2 inches . . . . 2 L = 20x20x5 cm
9x9x2 inches . . . . . . 2.5 L = 23x23x5 cm

Rectangular
13x9x2 inches . . . . . 3.5 L = 33x23x5 cm

Loaf
9x5x3 inches . . . . 2 L = 23x13x7 cm

Round
8x1½ inches . . . . 1.2 L = 20x4 cm
9x1½ inches . . . . 1.5 L = 23x4 cm

Recipe Abbreviations

t. = teaspoon. . . . . ltr. = liter
T. = tablespoon. . . . . oz. = ounce
c. = cup. . . . . lb. = pound
pt. = pint. . . . . .doz. = dozen
qt. = quart. . . . . .pkg. = package
gal. = gallon. . . . . .env. = envelope

Oven Temperatures

300° F. . . . . .150° C
325° F. . . . . .160° C
350° F. . . . . .180° C
375° F. . . . . .190° C
400° F. . . . . .200° C
450° F. . . . . .230° C

Kitchen Measurements

A pinch = ⅛ tablespoon
1 fluid ounce = 2 tablespoons
3 teaspoons = 1 tablespoon
4 fluid ounces = ½ cup
2 tablespoons = ⅛ cup
8 fluid ounces = 1 cup
4 tablespoons = ¼ cup
16 fluid ounces = 1 pint
8 tablespoons = ½ cup
32 fluid ounces = 1 quart
16 tablespoons = 1 cup
16 ounces net weight = 1 pound
2 cups = 1 pint
4 cups = 1 quart
4 quarts = 1 gallon

Send us your favorite recipe

and the memory that makes it special for you!*

If we select your recipe for a brand-new **Gooseberry Patch** cookbook, your name will appear right along with it...and you'll receive a FREE copy of the book!

Submit your recipe on our website at

www.gooseberrypatch.com/sharearecipe

*Please include the number of servings and all other necessary information.

Have a taste for more?

Visit www.gooseberrypatch.com to join our Circle of Friends!

• Free recipes, tips and ideas plus a complete cookbook index
• Get mouthwatering recipes and special email offers delivered to your inbox.

You'll also love these cookbooks from **Gooseberry Patch**!

A Year of Holidays
The Best Instant Pot® Cookbook
Fresh Farmhouse Recipes
From Grandma's Recipe Box
Grandma's Best Comfort Foods
Mom's Go-To Recipes
Our Best Farm-Fresh Recipes
Our Best Quick & Easy Casseroles
Quick & Easy Recipes for Gatherings
Smart & Easy Meal Planning

www.gooseberrypatch.com